DATE DUE			

Rural Versus Urban Political Power

DISCARDED

RURAL VERSUS URBAN POLITICAL POWER

The ·Nature and Consequences of Unbalanced Representation

By GORDON E. BAKER

University of California, Santa Barbara College

GREENWOOD PRESS, PUBLISHERS

WESTPORT, CONNECTICUT

Library of Congress Cataloging in Publication Data

Baker, Gordon E
    Rural versus urban political power.

    Reprint of the ed. published by Doubleday,
Garden City, N. Y., which was issued as no. 20
of Doubleday short studies in political science.
    Bibliography: p.
    1.   Election districts--United States.
2.   United States--Politics and government--20th
century.   I.   Title.
[JK1982.B3   1979]   328.73'07'345   78-12263
ISBN 0-313-21223-6

Reprinted with the permission of Random House, Inc.

Reprinted in 1979 by Greenwood Press, Inc.,
51 Riverside Avenue, Westport, CT 06880

Printed in the United States of America

10 9 8 7 6 5 4 3 2 1

Editor's Foreword

Professor Baker has helped measurably to fill another gap in the literature of political science. The relationships and tensions between urban and rural political power comprise a vital and lively aspect of American politics. In view of the long-standing problems and the unlikelihood that conditions will be altered basically in the foreseeable future, this carefully organized and reasoned study should be of lasting value. The struggle of cities to overcome the effects of unbalanced representation is headline material, but for the student of politics certain fundamental issues are raised. Fortunately, Professor Baker has analyzed urban and rural representation as something more than a source of current controversy. He has related it to the nation's political traditions, to its social environment, and to democratic theory. Aside from questions of principle, the developments described illustrate graphically the impact of social change on the political process.

The way in which the various jurisdictional boundaries of units of government became established in the United States is a fascinating story in itself. Nonetheless, it is with the long-run consequences of unchanging boundaries that this essay is concerned. A continuing social and technological revolution has tended to undermine whatever good sense and functional need was embodied in original political units. It is a well-known fact that rural areas, for example, no longer contain the numbers of people and the economic bases of government which they once did. With the concentration of population and business enterprise, the urban centers of political life are much more significant than their control over political decisions which affect them reflects. It is also true, as the author amply demonstrates, that marked social change has not produced proportionate revision of jurisdictions and formal procedures for representation. Older representational practices have become hopelessly outdated. In this respect at least, the American political system has developed hardening of the arteries. Why? If the overwhelming numbers of citizens and economic interests are in effect underrepresented at the state and national levels of government, why are new rules not devised? Doubtless inertia and the heavy yet invisible hand of the past have something to do with it. The whole explanation runs to the heart of some of the basic conditions of American politics as the following pages suggest.

While vaguely aware that cities are occasionally starved for necessary funds because of the preponderant power of rural areas in the state legislature and that ancient boundaries produce bizarre situations, it is likely that the average citizen has not tallied up the total cost of unbalanced representation. One of Professor Baker's most useful contributions is to summarize the factual evidence and to show how broad and serious are the consequences. One reason perhaps for the failure to reapportion all·along the line is that urban dwellers are only hit with immediate effects in isolated cases. The outstanding case of New York City, detailed by the author, indicates that the day may have arrived when the city-dweller pays a continuous high price for the political heritage from colonial times.

Often brief treatments of the problems of rural-urban balance are confined to the more glaring examples on the state and local level. This study includes equally penetrating analysis of the problem at the national level. Unfortunately, the matter is not simply one of amassing evidence of the blatant inequities in political representation, of the lack of correspondence between jurisdictional units on the one hand and revenue sources and needs on the other. A clear-cut proof of irrationality might be convincing were it not for the fact that other values enter in. Area representation (as distinct from population representation) also flows from and protects an American tradition. Fear of possible urban tyranny is still a force. Rural America continues to embody—as a symbol and, to many, in actuality—enduring human virtues. To raise head-on the question of unbalanced rural representation would be to raise a moral question as well. Furthermore, in certain areas, one or the other of the two parties has a vested interest in the *status quo* if its political strength happens to rest on a predominantly rural vote.

Beyond the issues of practical politics and ethics, there are issues which arise from democratic theory and American political values. After examining the causes, extent, and results of rural-urban unbalance, Professor Baker interprets his findings in the light of our federal system, the ever-present insistence upon states' rights, the principle of equality of representation and majority rule, and the conflict between majority rule and minority rights. Here practice is sharply contrasted with theory. At this point, the study centers on the way political institutions do or do not express certain values which the society is agreed are important and on the sometimes unintended consequences of various arrangements. His critical analysis provides a basis in the final chapter for a consideration of remedies.

Professor Baker has proven that compact short studies, chosen with imagination and on the basis of an appreciation for what is crucial in politics and rigorously presented, can have multiple value. Here is a particular problem of American politics—important in itself—discussed in such a way that several aspects of political science are illuminated in the process.

RICHARD C. SNYDER

Contents

CHAPTER ONE

Our Rural Heritage and Urban Society

Those who labor in the earth are the chosen people of God,
if ever He had a chosen people, whose breasts He has made
His peculiar deposit for substantial and genuine virtue. . . .
The mobs of great cities add just so much to the support of
pure government, as sores do to the strength of the human
body.

— THOMAS JEFFERSON

This sentiment, expressed by early America's greatest democrat, is of
more than historical interest. It has symbolized an enduring part of this
nation's heritage. The virtues of agrarian life have always had an enormous appeal to the average American. Even many city dwellers, themselves usually no more than a generation or two removed from the farm,
tend to look upon urban life with suspicion.

In spite of the fact that the United States has become predominantly
urban during the twentieth century, the image of rural virtues and of the
superiority of rural life persists. The shift over the past generation from
a rural to an urban society has taken place here so rapidly—almost
suddenly—that attitudes have understandably lagged. Thus the traditional American ideal of the virtuous, self-reliant farmer with his roots
in the soil has given much public opinion an uncritical bias. The city
has been regarded as the source of corruption and immorality, while the
countryside supposedly preserves the virtues of honesty, thrift, and character. Farmers, we are often reminded, constitute the very "backbone of
democracy."

How realistic are such stereotypes? The indictment against city life
generally stresses political corruption and notorious bossism; implicit also
is a distasteful view of some adverse effects of industrialization upon cities:
congestion, slums, and crime—conditions inevitably contrasted with the
imagined bucolic splendor and innocence of agrarian life. This picture,
however, is one-sided. While cities are open to some blame upon all of
these scores, they can proudly boast of some uniquely urban contributions
to society, notably the fostering of cultural activities and of intellectual

1

and social freedom. Also ignored by many is the fact that slums are by no means confined to cities. Decaying rural areas are often deficient in both material and cultural advantages. A. Whitney Griswold, President of Yale University, has observed: "A self-sufficient farm in our time is more likely to be a haunt of illiteracy and malnutrition than a wellspring of democracy."[1]

On the political side of rural-urban differences are two additional factors worth stressing. One is that civic reform movements and governmental reorganization have made enormously greater strides over the past half century in cities than on either the county or state level. Second, political machines and bosses are by no means confined to urban areas. Rural machines are less colorful or dramatic and far less publicized, but their existence and power cannot be ignored. Professor Lane Lancaster, a lifelong student of rural government, attests that:

> It is safe to say that in nine-tenths of the counties in the United States public affairs are in the hands of what the irreverent call the "court-house gang." . . . The doings of the gang are perhaps not so dramatic as the gorgeous pillagings of a Tweed . . . and they have certainly not had as good a press, but no veteran need feel diffident in the presence of his urban brethren.[2]

Population Growth and Trends

The foregoing paragraphs might seem little more than interesting sociological observations were it not for the fact that the conflict between urban and rural interests is in fact a far-reaching and increasingly important struggle for power in American politics—national, state, and local. For, while urbanization continues at a rapid pace, our political institutions more often than not reflect patterns from the rural past.

Some notion of the dramatic transformation of American society over the past half century can be gleaned from a glance at population trends. At the close of the nineteenth century we were still predominantly a rural nation, but the rise of the city was already challenging the traditional patterns. As the old frontier of the wilderness vanished from the scene, a new and different urban frontier took its place. A steadily increasing flow of population from farm to city began. The turn of the century in 1900 found three-fifths of all Americans still living on farms or in rural communities of fewer than 2,500 inhabitants (the United States census breakpoint for the urban-rural distinction). But between 1910 and 1930 the proportion nearly reversed itself, with over 56 per cent of the nation's population classified as urban in the 1930 census. This nearly approached the saturation point as far as many cities were concerned, for the main trends of population movement since 1930 have been in suburban areas outside city limits. The 1950 census recognized this development by extending its classification to include as urban the densely settled (but often unincorporated) fringe areas surrounding cities of 50,000 or more inhabitants. That the urbanizing trend is continuing is seen in the 1950 census counts, which classified 64 per cent of the nation's population as urban. Approximately 70 per cent of this city population is concentrated in large municipal areas of 50,000 or more inhabitants. The widespread nature of this growth is shown by the fact that thirty states have more urban than rural inhabitants.

Urbanism and Representation

Despite this dramatic shift in the make-up of American society, certain older political patterns have persisted, causing increasing stresses and strains. For instance, the vast ecological changes have not been matched by comparable changes in territorial units of government, notably the county. Notwithstanding the revolutionary advances in technology, communications, and transportation, the pattern of county units established by the end of the nineteenth century has remained largely impervious to change. Territorial boundaries created in a far different era have, with minor and scattered exceptions, persisted until the present. But while many counties have declined as realistic and adequate geographical units, they continue to serve as the basic political units for state politics. Legislative districts have likewise tended to survive unchanged the transformations in both population and general political sentiment.

Specifically, the static character of formal territorial units in the face of politically significant population shifts has resulted in an increasingly crucial problem—the nature of legislative representation. While urban areas have grown to a predominant position in terms of numbers, their political role has generally remained subordinate. Rural dominance was natural and logical in the nineteenth century, so long as the nation was largely agrarian. But the failure of state representative bodies to reflect the changing character of society has resulted in a number of problems for a modern industrialized age.

In most states at the present time the urban citizen is accorded much less political weight than the rural or small-town resident. According to the principle of political equality, all legislators should represent approximately equal numbers of citizens. Yet the average city constituency is usually considerably more populous than the typical rural or small-town district. For example, a city representative may speak for upwards of 50,000 persons, while a rural legislator may represent only 10,000 or 20,000. On a state-wide basis, such discrepancies leave city dwellers in a far weaker political position than rural constituents. The result is minority rule by artificially created legislative majorities. The United States Conference of Mayors has estimated that the nation's substantial majority of urbanites pay 90 per cent of all taxes, but receive on a national average only 25 per cent of state legislative representation.

As a result of this situation, a strategic political advantage is enjoyed by powerful groups in a position to profit by a distortion of representation. Nor are these groups entirely rural in make-up. Certain conservative city forces actually fear equitable political strength for their own localities on the ground that the status quo is more safely ensured under the formal control of "less radical" country legislators. These interested groups, whether rural or urban (or in combination) are often able to retain their advantage by capitalizing upon the traditional pro-rural bias in public attitudes mentioned earlier.

The Jeffersonian Heritage

Those who resist greater representative strength for urban citizens seldom fail to invoke Jefferson's praise of small landholders and his hope that America would not develop large city mobs as in the Europe of his day. Such references are hardly relevant today. The independent yeomanry of the eighteenth century has largely disappeared and its remnants are generally uninfluential politically. The industrial revolution created both rural and urban patterns never envisaged by Jefferson.

It might be more meaningful to recall Jefferson's views on representation, a subject of vital significance to the democratic theory he helped develop. He consistently demanded a standard of equality for all citizens; representatives, he believed, should be apportioned throughout the state in accordance with the number of inhabitants in each area. Jefferson periodically criticized his own state's constitution for permitting inequality in representation, which he felt to be a matter of crucial importance. When Maine became a state in 1819, her constitution met Jefferson's approval in all respects except for the proviso that each town, regardless of size, be granted a seat in the legislature. This, he insisted, sacrificed "the equal rights of the people at large . . . to the privileges of a few." He added: "Equal representation is so fundamental a principle in a true republic that no prejudices can justify its violation because the prejudices themselves cannot be justified."[3]

With this in mind, let us next examine the relationship between democracy and representation.

CHAPTER TWO

The Theory of Equal Representation:
One Man, One Vote

> Equality of representation in the lawmaking tax levying bodies is a fundamental requisite of a free government, and no unbiased, fair, or just man has any right to claim a greater share of the voting power of the people than is granted to every other man similarly situated. It is vain for the people to hope for reforms of abuses or righteous results in legislation if the legislative bodies are not fairly representative of the spirit, purpose, and will of all the people, without discrimination.[1]

The above assertion by a state jurist is a concise summation of the theory of equal representation—a theory based upon the moral equality of all persons in a free government. It is usual to think of the principle of equality as a bar against discrimination upon grounds of race, creed, or social class. To these we might add locality. For what can justify allotting an inferior role to citizens merely because they live in certain geographical areas?

One of the basic assumptions of democratic rule is the doctrine of political equality. "One man, one vote" has been the most concise and effective phrase employed to illustrate the ideal that all citizens should have approximately the same political weight. This means that representative assemblies should reflect fairly accurately the character of the body politic. After all, of how much value is equal suffrage if all votes are not weighed equally? A concomitant feature of the right to vote is the right to have the vote counted—and counted as a full vote. Any considerable distortion in the representative picture means a dilution of some votes—in effect, a restriction on suffrage.

Yet an examination of American political institutions today reveals a situation of widespread inequality of representation. Most legislatures are so constituted that they do not faithfully reflect the "spirit, purpose, and will of all the people, without discrimination." The average urban resident's vote for the state legislature (and often for Congress as well) is diluted in comparison with that of the rural or small-town voter.

Not only is a situation of inequality prevalent, but it is vigorously defended in some quarters. Arguments usually given in defense of unequal representation tend to emphasize the professed dangers of majority rule. Even though all state governments are characterized by systems of checks and balances, some persons contend that even further checks are needed—checks specifically aimed at the growing urban majorities. In addition, there is usually an implicit assumption that rural citizens are more virtuous and less corrupt than those who live in cities. As was mentioned in the first chapter, this feeling of rural superiority has enjoyed a widespread appeal, in spite of its dubious validity. Defenders of unequal representative institutions also insist that a legislature should represent the interests of geographic sections and areas in addition to (or instead of) mere numbers of inhabitants. This theory presupposes that geographic boundaries such as counties or legislative districts denote socio-political communities of interest—an assumption that is open to serious question.

If we regard equal representation as the logical extension of the ideal of political equality, we might next ask how it is that the prevailing practice deviates so markedly from democratic theory. A brief historical analysis may indicate the development and strength of the egalitarian concept of representation, as well as some reasons for the general failure of contemporary legislatures to embody that theory.

Development of Equal Representation in England

The concept of political equality under representative government is a relatively recent one. The British House of Commons, the "Mother of Parliaments," had its origins in a feudal rather than a democratic society. At the outset the Commons represented localities rather than individuals. Counties and boroughs sent delegates to deal with the king on behalf of the various communities. The size of the constituency was irrelevant. With the breakdown of feudal society and the eventual emergence of a philosophy more concerned with individualism and eventually with equality, difficulties arose. The older representative pattern persisted in the face of fluid and changing conditions. The result was a "rotten borough" parliament. The "rotten boroughs" were constituencies which had become insignificant in population and importance, but which continued to be represented as before in Commons. At the same time thriving cities such as Manchester and Birmingham had come into prominence with no representation at all.

Indeed, a few boroughs had even become entirely depopulated, but still had seats in the legislature. A classic example was Old Sarum, with no inhabitants and two representatives, the same number that represented nearly a million persons in Yorkshire. Since no residence requirement existed, "rotten boroughs" still sent members to Parliament. The owners of the land could dispense seats much like patronage, and boroughs were bought, sold, and inherited. By 1793 an estimated eighty-four individuals controlled 157 seats in Commons, while a majority of that body was returned by fewer than 15,000 electors. Not until 1832 were the worst inequalities among districts removed, while a proper urban-rural balance was attained even later. The inception of modern British democracy can be dated from the Great Reform Act of 1832, with its constitutional principle that representation bears a direct relationship to population.

American Ideas and Experience

Colonial Period. In view of this English background, it is not surprising that representation in colonial America was originally based on localities. The isolated nature of early settlements, plus a high degree of autonomy in local communities and a similarity to each other in their make-up, provided a natural basis for representation by town. Far from being considered as a right, representation in the early colonial period was a duty, often fulfilled with reluctance. In 1670 Virginia levied a fine of 10,000 pounds of tobacco for any county failing to send two burgesses to the assembly. Massachusetts also assessed fines on delinquent towns.

However, the theory of political equality gradually developed. Frontier conditions and isolation from Europe created a much more fertile soil for its growth here than in the England of that time. As colonial unrest grew over the lack of representation in the British Parliament, an internal struggle was also taking place between the older coastal commercial settlements and the rapidly expanding, more democratic frontier groups. The western counties chafed under their inferior political status in the councils of most colonies. Threats of armed violence by frontiersmen in Pennsylvania resulted in provisions for a just apportionment of representatives in that commonwealth's constitution of 1776, which stated that "representation in proportion to the number of taxable inhabitants is the only principle which can at all times secure liberty, and make the voice of a majority of the people the law of the land."

In his "Notes on Virginia," written during the American Revolution, Thomas Jefferson pointed to two chief defects in his state's constitution. One consisted of restrictions on suffrage. The second: "Among those who share the representation, the shares are very unequal. Thus the county of Warwick, with one-hundred fighting men, has an equal representation with the county of Loudon, which has one thousand seven hundred and forty-six. So that every man in Warwick has as much influence in the government as seventeen in Loudon."[2] Jefferson proposed a model constitution, with legislative representation based on the number of qualified electors.

In some parts of New England the right of every town, regardless of size, to send a delegate to the legislature was brought into question. In 1777 a convention from Essex County declared misrepresentation to be the chief defect in a proposed constitution for Massachusetts. The group issued a document setting forth the democratic ideal of political equality —"The rights of representation should be so equally and impartially distributed, that the representatives should have the same views and interests with the people at large. . . . Let the representatives be apportioned among the respective counties, in proportion to their number of freemen."[3]

Revolution and Constitution.   It is clear that the question of representation took on crucial importance in the revolutionary atmosphere of the later eighteenth century. It is scarcely necessary to note the importance of this issue in the ultimate withdrawal of the thirteen American colonies from the British Empire. The Declaration of Independence stressed democratic ideals of equality and the right of representation. As is often the case, however, political institutions lagged behind the predominant theory of the day, so that political equality was far from complete in practice. All of the new states at the outset restricted suffrage through property qualifications, a situation which helped delay the development of the equitable representative patterns so widely advocated.

When delegates gathered in 1787 to create a new constitution for the United States, the smaller states were reluctant to yield their accustomed equality of status with the large—a status granted as a matter of convenience and necessity under the war-born Articles of Confederation. Yet the democratic ideal of representation as a substitute for direct action of the people was strong. Early in the debates James Wilson announced: "The doctrine of Representation is this—first the representative ought to speak the language of his Constituents, and secondly that his language or vote should have the same influence as though the Constituents gave it."[4] James Madison added that the states "ought to vote in the same proportion in which their citizens would do, if the people of all the States were collectively met."[5] In spite of the force of this argument, it soon became apparent that no federation would be possible without a concession to the small states. As a result, the principle of direct representation was modified by the creation of a senate with equal membership from the constituent states.

New States and New Problems.   Settlement of the question of representation on the federal level did not end the struggle in America over the problem. Within the various states, controversy persisted between the democratic frontier elements and the tidewater aristocracy, factions that had temporarily been united under the popular banners of the Revolution. The rapidly growing western sections felt that they were being exploited by the older and wealthier eastern areas, especially in regard to discriminatory and harsh taxation. It was not surprising that the interior should blame the twin obstacles of restricted suffrage and inequitable representation in the legislatures.

As new states (such as Kentucky and Tennessee) were formed along the frontier, their constitutions reflected some of this popular ferment. Also embodying the democratic theory of representation was the Northwest Ordinance of 1787, which provided the framework for the future organization of government in the vast region beyond the Appalachian mountains. The Ordinance specifically stipulated that "The inhabitants of the said territory shall always be entitled to the benefits of the writs of habeas corpus and of the trial by jury, of a proportionate representation of the people in the legislature, and of judicial proceedings according to the course of the common law." This would indicate that the subject of representation enjoyed something more than a trivial status.

In the older states the period from 1820 to 1840 witnessed a rapid extension of popular power, as one constitution after another underwent revision. While the struggle for political equality centered primarily on suffrage restrictions, it often involved the question of representation as well, since conservatives generally sought to retain at least an upper house representing the propertied interests. State after state, however, yielded to the advance of democracy; property qualifications were abandoned and white manhood suffrage was largely achieved by the 1830s. In regard to representation there was no definite pattern, though the trend in newly formed western states was generally democratic in adhering to a population standard. Some states with large areas and few inhabitants took account of territory as well as people, but these deviations were often more accidental than designed.

A stress on localities persisted in some older states, especially in New England, but even here the traditional prerevolutionary practice of town representation was challenged. A successful fight for a change in the historic pattern took place in Massachusetts, where small-town dominance evoked controversy at the state constitutional convention of 1853. There Charles Francis Adams contended: "I maintain that the moment a majority in a republic assumes to draw a distinction with the intent that certain men shall be enabled to enjoy twice or thrice the amount of political power which an equal number of other men are to possess, that is the hour when tyranny begins."[6] Within a few years the theory enunciated by Adams prevailed and the equal district system replaced town representation.

Toward the end of the nineteenth century a distrust of growing cities resulted in restrictions on urban power. This indicated a reversal of the late-eighteenth-century condition of underrepresented frontier and agrarian areas. One explanation for this curious turn-about is that threats to the status quo had largely shifted from rural to urban groups. The rise of cities in the nineteenth century caused the emergence of a large class of property-less laborers, whose enfranchisement alarmed men of substance, both rural and urban. After losing the battles over an extended suffrage, conservatives in a number of states sought to neutralize its effects by controlling the apportionment of legislative representatives.

An emphasis on localities, together with the failure of lawmaking bodies to reapportion seats according to population shifts, have always resulted in distortions from democratic standards. In an earlier day of relative sim-plicity and homogeneity, these discrepancies were less significant. But in an era of phenomenal population changes, the gap between theory and prac-tice has become especially wide. By the middle of the twentieth century the pattern of state legislative representation reveals sharp disadvantages to growing urban areas, while declining rural districts enjoy a political power based on an importance long since gone. While no examples in any state quite match the fame of England's Old Sarum, many are not far removed. The term "rotten boroughs," which originally referred to a feudal anachronism, is becoming an increasingly apt descriptive term for many American state electoral districts today.

Urban-Rural Imbalance at the State Level

In 1955 inequality of legislative representation is solidly entrenched in all but a handful of the forty-eight states. Most urban areas are discriminated against in at least one house of their state legislature, and in many cases in both houses. This situation can be explained by two major causes —constitutional provisions and legislative failure to reapportion properly.

Reasons for Unbalanced Representation

Constitutional Restrictions on Populous Areas. In the first place, a number of state constitutions provide for representation of area regardless of population. This takes various forms. Extreme cases are the town representation provisions for the lower houses of the legislatures in Vermont and Connecticut. In the latter state, Hartford's 177,397 residents send two representatives, as does Union town, with a population of only 261. In Vermont, 49 inhabitants of Victory town enjoy the same share of the lower house as Burlington's 33,155. Similar distortions are evident in the seven states (New Jersey, Idaho, South Carolina, Montana, New Mexico, Arizona, and Nevada) that allow each county, large or small, one seat in the state senate. California modifies this arrangement only slightly by combining some of the smallest counties into senate districts. Some resulting distortions from democratic theory are seen in these examples:

Rural Sussex County's 34,423 inhabitants, and metropolitan Essex County's 905,949 each send one senator to the New Jersey legislature.

Los Angeles County's 4,151,687 people receive the same senate representation as 14,014 in the senate district composed of Mono, Inyo, and Alpine counties in the Sierra Nevada mountains.

Other frequent methods of limiting larger urban areas are: formulas and ratios which allow progressively less representation to more populous communities; provisions against dividing counties into districts; minimum representation for each county; maximum limits for populous counties and cities. For instance, Iowa's constitution ensures a double advantage to rural areas by limiting any one county to a single senator and by guaranteeing a representative to each of the state's 99 counties, regardless of size. Since the lower house is limited to 108 seats, the restrictive ceiling on the nine most populous counties is obvious.

In a number of cases constitutional barriers are an accidental remnant from apparently convenient arrangements in the eighteenth and nineteenth centuries, set before the growth of urban centers resulted in an increasingly undemocratic situation. In an earlier day when population was spread less unevenly and the total number of counties in a state remained fairly small, provisions for minimum representation could be justified. Later on, however, shrewd politicians in some states found a handy advantage in creating many additional counties as a means of increasing legislative strength. Also, special limitations on the growing populous areas became frequent as rural forces modified constitutions in many states while they could still command a majority.

As a result, by 1955 there were only twelve states with no constitutional restrictions of any consequence upon a democratic pattern of representation in both houses. These are: Washington, North Dakota, South Dakota, Nebraska, Minnesota, Wisconsin, Indiana, Illinois, Tennessee, Massachusetts, Virginia and Colorado. Except for the last two (whose constitutions are silent or vague) these states specifically require representation to be based on total population, or legal voters, or adult male population. This does not mean, of course, that legislatures in all of these states follow the constitutional stipulations. In several additional states, restrictions on equal districting are reasonably moderate in their over-all effect. In other cases, a more realistic arrangement of counties could overcome existing inequities. However, it is safe to say that the attainment of equitable representative systems in at least half the forty-eight states awaits constitutional change.

Legislative Failure to Reapportion.   A second—though less extensive—cause of unrepresentative state legislatures is the failure of the lawmaking bodies to keep districting arrangements abreast of population changes. Most state constitutions call for periodic reapportionment of one or both houses, usually after every federal census. This requirement, however, is often more honored in the breach than in the observance. Framers of state constitutions were wise in providing for future shifts in representation to keep pace with newer population patterns; but they were either optimistic or naive in leaving such a function to the very body affected by the change.

This unhappy fact has been demonstrated convincingly by the record in all but a few states, so that even when there have been no constitutional barriers to democratic representation, inequalities have resulted from legislative inaction. Tennessee elects a lawmaking body that reflects population patterns of 1900. Minnesota's present apportionment dates back to 1913, Indiana's to 1921. Washington last reapportioned in 1930, and then only when an aroused urban electorate employed the popular initiative to overcome thirty years of inaction by the legislature. Failure to reapportion is the sole source of inequitable representation in six states and contributes substantially (in addition to constitutional restrictions) to a distorted picture in about ten more.

Since reapportionment has been so frequently stipulated in state constitutions, one might assume that these requirements could be enforced. However, numerous appeals have found state courts traditionally reluctant to interfere with the legislatures, even though judges have consistently held that reapportionment is a "mandatory duty." While the judiciary has not hesitated to invalidate positive acts of malapportionment (especially when flagrant abuses of legislative discretion are evident), it has left untouched the more serious negative process of "silent gerrymandering" caused by inaction. Judicial caution is partially understandable, since forcing a coordinate branch of government to perform a positive constitutional duty is more difficult than merely invalidating an unconstitutional act. However, it does seem that a problem so crucial to the very basis of government might have impelled courts to find ways of enforcing legislative obligations. Requiring intransigent legislators to be elected from the state at large (a prospect that is anathema to all politicans) would have been one method of encouraging a speedy adherence to the constitution. Another might have been to consider an un-reapportioned legislature competent to pass only one law—a reapportionment act. Indeed, the Louisiana constitution of 1845 (in a section long since repealed) actually stipulated that after every census no law should be passed until a new apportionment was made. However interesting such speculations may be, they offer little practical hope that a thoroughly established precedent of judicial nonenforcement will be overturned.

The reasons for such a widespread failure of legislatures to live up to state constitutional redistricting requirements are not difficult to find. In almost any reapportionment a number of legislators would be personally affected through the abolition or consolidation of districts. A legislator naturally finds the status quo under which he was elected to be satisfactory and usually dreads the prospect of a new and unknown constituency. Also, many refuse to move because their particular party would lose strength. In almost all cases a dominant consideration has been the increasing disparities in rural and urban popular strength, with legislators from smaller communities showing a hostility to growing cities. Finally, interest groups benefiting from the status quo have fought reapportionment.

A point deserving emphasis is the fact that while opposition to reapportionment is more frequent among rural legislators, not all of their city colleagues are eager for a change. While urban areas have consistently outgained rural regions in population, these gains do not occur evenly within cities. Within some large urban areas, many districts gain at the expense of others. For example, Cook County (Chicago) has for decades been grossly underrepresented in a rural-dominated state legislature. Yet until 1955 the five smallest and hence most overrepresented districts were not found, as might be expected, in the downstate region, but were located in declining areas of Chicago. Cook County districts varied in size from 39,368 to 700,325.

One further motive for legislative refusal to reapportion has been to force a change in the state constitution from a democratic standard to one favoring declining areas. In some states long periods of legislative refusal to honor the existing constitution brought results. Large municipalities were persuaded to yield their sound but neglected claims to equal representation for a disadvantageous arrangement that would at least guarantee a periodic reapportionment in one house. Their relative strength in the other house has usually been greatly reduced. This is often termed a "balance" plan, which means that several heavy weights are thrown on the rural side of the scales.

In return for these concessions, urban districts are usually assured of an "automatic" scheme that vests reapportionment of the one representative house in the hands of an executive officer or commission, either in the first instance or in the event of legislative inaction. This permits judicial enforcement. California and Michigan are among the states that have adopted this type of solution after years of bitter struggle. In other states where apportionment is a serious problem a similar "compromise" is often advocated—and sometimes accepted even by weary urban reform groups despairing of ever obtaining constitutional justice. In 1954, Illinois (where a rural-dominated legislature had refused to obey the constitution for over half a century) discarded democratic provisions for representation in favor of a "balanced" scheme. Here the citizens of Chicago were faced with the dilemma of either retaining their strong moral and constitutional claim to equality (which had been ignored) or approving a proposed amendment to the state constitution that ensured an enforced reapportionment of one house on a population basis but placed permanent control of the state senate in the down-state region.

While the experience of states in which one house of the legislature represents people and the other house pastures has hardly justified optimism or confidence, there has been a definite trend in recent years toward the adoption of "balanced" schemes. Some of these give a padded weight to area in both houses, but more especially in the upper chamber. New Mexico in 1949, Nevada in 1950 and Arizona in 1953 have all changed their constitutions to allow each county (most of them sparsely settled) the same weight in the state senate. A misleading but apparently persuasive case put forward by rural interests was that such an arrangement parallels the pattern of the United States Senate. California, which in 1928 abandoned constitutional provisions for democratic representation that had gone unenforced, adopted the misnomer "Federal Plan" for its reconstituted legislature. Here, as elsewhere, it was suggested that counties within the state should be regarded as states are in the Union, despite the fact that counties are merely legal agents which the state creates for administrative purposes. All states are unitary rather than federal in internal make-up. And, in most instances, there is scant public feeling of a distinct community of interests bounded by county lines. Illogical as the federal analogy is—legally, theoretically, and practically—it often gains an uncritical acceptance.

Extent of Unbalanced Representation

The above reasons, then, have contributed to the current situation of urban underrepresentation in state legislatures. What is the extent of rural advantage throughout the nation, and what is its degree of intensity? Answers to these questions can be furnished in large part by data revealed in Table 1 on pages 16 and 17. For this purpose the principal urban areas in each state have been studied from the standpoint of the relation which their population bears to their representative strength in each house of the legislature. While this method cannot divulge a complete picture in any state, it can provide a concise and graphic outline of the way in which representative patterns affect urban political power. In nearly all states, of course, the total urban population is considerably greater than the percentage listed for the selected areas. However, for statistical purposes there are numerous advantages in using only the larger cities in most states. Smaller municipalities are often located in larger districts with substantial rural populations, thus complicating an estimate of legislative strength. Moreover, the most populous urban areas in each state generally receive the main brunt of the discriminatory patterns.

Categories of States. In order to focus more clearly on the extent and degree of urban underrepresentation, the forty-eight states listed in Table 1 are grouped into five separate categories. In group V are the only two states that provide an unmistakable pattern of representative equality for urban citizens. Group IV contains seven states whose urban districts are only moderately underrepresented. In group III the situation is slightly more serious. Group II includes the bulk of states, twenty-two in number, where distortions from democratic theory can be considered substantial. Finally, group I is reserved for eight states where the situation seems especially severe.

Of the few states allowing urban populations a proportionate voice in the legislature, Massachusetts comes closest to the ideal of "one man, one vote." Districts for both houses follow a relatively equal population pattern with amazing consistency. Representation is based upon the distribution

TABLE 1

Representation of Principal Urban Areas

States	Selected urban areas	Per cent of state population	Per cent of lower house	Per cent of senate
		GROUP I—SEVERE		
Georgia	6 largest urban counties	32	9	7
Florida	9 most urban counties	60	23	24
Delaware	Wilmington urbanized area	59	23	24
Maryland	Baltimore & 3 largest urban counties	67	44	31
Connecticut	10 largest cities	46	7	46[a]
Rhode Island	10 largest cities	77	67	34
New Jersey	8 largest urban counties	75	73	38
California	4 largest urban counties	59	59	10
		GROUP II		
New York	New York City	53	43	43
Kansas	3 largest urban counties	26	7	8
Alabama	3 largest urban counties	30	13	9
Iowa	5 largest urban counties	24	10	10
Oklahoma	2 largest urban counties	26	12	6
Texas	4 largest urban counties	29	19	13
Minnesota	2 largest urban counties	35	23	22
New Mexico	largest urban county	21	11	3
Tennessee	4 largest urban counties	38	22	20
Arizona	2 largest urban counties	62	62	7
Nevada	2 largest urban counties	62	40	12
Michigan	Wayne County	38	35	21
Missouri	St. Louis & 2 largest urban counties	45	25	41
Illinois	Chicago	42	39	31
Ohio	8 largest urban counties	54	39	54
South Carolina	3 largest urban counties	22	22	7
Vermont	entire urban population	36	6	36[a]
Idaho	4 largest urban counties	28	19	9
North Dakota	4 largest cities	17	12	10
Montana	5 largest urban counties	37	32	9
North Carolina	4 largest counties	22	16	16[a]
Mississippi	2 largest urban counties	10	4	4
		GROUP III		
Utah	3 largest urban counties	64	48	48
Indiana	6 largest urban counties	46	32	34
Washington	3 largest urban counties	52	44	48
Colorado	Denver city	31	26	23

States	Selected urban areas	Per cent of state population	Per cent of lower house	Per cent of senate
Oregon	largest urban county	31	27	23
Nebraska	2 largest urban counties	30		23
Kentucky	3 largest urban counties	23	17	18
Louisiana	3 largest urban parishes	34	26	26
Maine	8 largest cities	27	19	27[a]
GROUP IV—MODERATE				
Pennsylvania	2 largest urban counties	34	32	28
Virginia	8 largest cities & 4 largest urban counties	34	28	33
West Virginia	3 largest urban counties	21	19	12
Wyoming	5 most urban counties	48	41	33
South Dakota	6 largest urban counties	30	28	23
Arkansas	3 largest urban counties	16	12	14
New Hampshire	3 largest cities	27	25	29
GROUP V—EQUAL REPRESENTATION				
Wisconsin	3 largest urban counties	33	32	33
Massachusetts	All cities over 50,000 population	50	50	50[a]

Figures are rounded to nearest percentage
[a]Approximate

of legal voters instead of population, though the results would be much the same on either standard. The latest reapportionment in Massachusetts occurred in 1947 and 1948 following the state's decennial census of voters held in 1945. The districting arrangements have not, however, escaped the charge of being an unusually effective partisan gerrymander. Boundary lines are so drawn that the Republican Party has apparently benefited considerably in a close two-party state. However, the equitable weight given all urban areas is still a unique accomplishment.

Wisconsin's legislature, which had not been reapportioned for some thirty years, can finally claim—beginning in 1954—one of the most representative lawmaking bodies in the nation. While several distortions in district populations are made inevitable by constitutional restrictions against breaking county lines, most districts fall reasonably close to an ideal average. The few inequalities do not work to the disadvantage of urban areas. Reapportionment brought about substantial gains for both smaller and larger urban counties. The Milwaukee and Madison regions especially benefited from the change.

In a few states where Table 1 indicates an underrepresentation of urban districts the situation is less disadvantageous to city population than the figures might indicate. Wherever numerous delegates are elected at large from a county that contains rural as well as urban population, the city often tends to dominate the election because of its favorable position. This means that while the delegation may be underrepresented on the basis of a total percentage, the city viewpoint receives adequate support. Wyoming, West Virginia, South Dakota, and Arkansas are four rural states where larger districts as such are underrepresented; but the situation cannot correctly be considered as one of inadequate urban power. At-large elections help modify the degree of urban underrepresentation in Indiana and Utah as well.

Cities and Suburbs. As might be expected, the largest city within most states is the primary target of discriminatory representation. New York, Chicago, Los Angeles, St. Louis, Detroit, Baltimore, Atlanta, Birmingham, and Providence are all well-publicized examples. The list could be extended to include most principal cities. Notable exception to the rule are Boston, Milwaukee, New Orleans, Richmond, and Norfolk—all of which receive representation approximately equivalent to population. Moderately below strength are Philadelphia and Pittsburgh. It is interesting—and unusual— that underrepresentation in Virginia and Louisiana, while not extensive, is confined to medium-sized cities rather than to the principal ones.

In addition to cities proper, fast-growing suburban areas are often among the most severely underrepresented constituencies. As once-sparsely-settled districts increase in population many-fold, additional inequalities arise. For example, Baltimore city was originally the principal victim of Maryland's apportionment pattern. While the city's strength in the legislature is still far from adequate, even less proportionate weight is now held by suburban Baltimore County and the two flourishing counties that house many commuters from Washington, D.C. The most underrepresented areas in Pennsylvania prior to a reapportionment in 1953 were the suburbs surrounding Philadelphia. It is significant that political equality went long unnoticed by some state legislatures until growing suburban areas began to feel the pinch of inadequate representation. This is doubtless due to the fact that political sentiment in suburbia is generally conservative and often quite compatible with rural views on how the state should be governed. This would seem to be the main explanation behind the 1954 movement to amend the Illinois constitution in respect to representation. So long as Chicago proper was the primary victim of the situation, the rural-dominated legislature saw no need to obey constitutional provisions for reapportionment according to population. By 1954 the city as a whole was still underrepresented, but far less than nearby suburban territory. Politically, the city is Democratic, while both suburban Cook County and downstate Illinois are largely Republican. In 1953 a Republican governor managed to persuade a Republican legislature to propose a constitutional amendment for a "balanced" area-population scheme of representation. Ratified by the electorate in 1954, the new basis of apportionment resulted in moderate gains in one house and moderate losses in the other for the city of Chicago. But suburban Cook County increased its representation enormously, gaining five times as much weight as formerly in one house and six times as much in the other. The total effect of the amendment was to leave the city underrepresented, while giving suburban Cook County legislative strength proportionate to its population. Downstate areas lost some strength, but remained overrepresented in the senate.

Consequences of Unbalanced Representation

On the Two-Party System. The far-reaching effects of rural legislative advantage are not always sufficiently appreciated. Whenever "rotten borough" situations have aroused publicity the problem is often treated in isolation, as though the controversy concerned only cities versus farmers. Such a view obscures the widespread ramifications of urban-rural representation. One of the most important effects of a distorted legislative pattern concerns the political party balance. In a number of states the party split bears a high correlation to the extent of urbanism. As a general rule, the Democratic Party in the North and West is stronger in city districts, while Republicans usually find most solid support in rural and suburban regions. However, in some border states—Oklahoma, Kentucky, Maryland, and Delaware are examples—Republican support is often weaker in rural than in urban and suburban areas. This is becoming increasingly true also in some parts of the South, though the real contests in that region result from Democratic intraparty differences, with liberal elements usually stronger in urban areas. In fact, the hard core of Southern conservatism lies in the rural "black belt," where a small white minority, grossly overrepresented in state legislatures as well as in other political institutions of the section, exercises enormous power.

With this general situation in mind, it is obvious that a representative system allowing urban areas less legislative strength than their populations merit gives an immediate advantage to the political party or faction that is stronger in smaller towns and rural areas. The imbalance varies from state to state, but it exists at least to some degree in most of them. This can result in legislative control by the actual minority party, even in states which vote heavily in the opposite direction. In other instances, even if the successful party represents a popular majority, its legislative strength is often greatly bloated due to a monopoly of rural seats. In New York the two-party struggle is closely contested, and state-wide offices might go to either party. But the state legislature has been termed "Republican by constitutional law." Since New York City is heavily Democratic and the upstate region largely Republican, the impact of city underrepresentation is apparent. When Chester Bowles became Democratic governor of Connecticut in 1949, his party held a 23 to 13 edge in the fairly representative state senate. But in the lower house, based on towns, the Republicans held a solid 180 to 92 majority. In 1950 party alignments in several selected states were as follows:

TABLE 2

State	Governor	Senate (Membership)		House	
		Dem.	Repub.	Dem.	Repub.
Illinois	Democratic	18	32	81	72
Michigan	Democratic	9	23	39	61
Montana	Democratic	23	31	55	35
Nevada	Democratic	6	11	25	18
Rhode Island	Democratic	22	22	64	35

The above table indicates sharp disparities between the political sentiment for the governorship and the partisan make-up of the legislative body. Since the state executive is chosen at large, his election is generally a more accurate index to popular feeling than the election of a legislature whose electoral districts are distorted for rural advantage. While many other reasons, including weak local organization, can also contribute to a disparity between a party's statewide and legislative strength, the above examples would seem to demonstrate the primary importance of disproportionate representation. In Montana, Nevada, and Rhode Island the Democratic Party claimed both the governorship and the more representative branch of the legislature, but the weighted rural vote was clearly felt in the misrepresentative upper house. Democrats have won nearly every state office in Rhode Island for over two decades, but have never controlled the town-dominated senate. The case of Michigan partially reflected the highly inadequate strength of the Detroit area in both houses. In Illinois, Adlai Stevenson swept the governor's office in 1948 by some 572,000 votes, but faced a predominantly Republican, downstate senate for his entire four-year term. Only a unique electoral system for the lower house enabled Democrats to overcome, in part, the effects of unequal districts. Interestingly enough, the Illinois "balanced" districting of 1954, carried under the banner of reform, perpetuated (and probably even strengthened) Republican control of the senate by virtually writing it into the state constitution.

In most examples of this type it is the Republican Party that enjoys the advantage due to its generally greater strength in rural areas outside the South. However, the tables can be turned in Maryland, where an unrepresentative pattern favors Democrats in the state legislature. A mushrooming suburban populace has enabled the Republican Party to elect two United States senators and a governor since 1950. Yet the state legislature seems beyond hope of capture. In 1951 the score was: senate—18 Democrats, 11 Republicans; house—88 Democrats, 35 Republicans.

Even in states where one party is traditionally dominant, disproportionate representation has contributed to weakening the opposition party still further. In Republican Iowa, Democrats show considerable state-wide strength, having taken some 44 per cent of the total vote for congressional candidates in 1950. This would seem to be a fair indication of potential minority strength. Yet, in that same year, Democrats could elect only 15 of 108 state representatives and 9 of 50 senators. In Democratic Florida, growing Republican strength enabled that party to poll over a quarter of the total vote in both the congressional and gubernatorial elections in 1952. But the northern influx of Republican voters to Florida's cities has made little dent on the state's heavily rural legislature. In 1952 Republicans could claim only 1 of 38 state senators and 5 of the 95 representatives.

The effect upon the two-party system within the states is surely one of the most telling indictments that can be brought against the condition of inflated rural power. The whole rationale of the two-party system is that it should offer alternative choices of candidates and programs to the electorate. In this way the parties give meaning and purpose to public sentiment and also serve to strengthen the element of responsibility among governing officials. Ideally, parties should contest for public support in such a way that votes can be translated into some sort of public policy. In a democracy there should be a reasonably direct relationship between predominant public opinion and the power to govern. With this in mind, the implications of a distorted pattern of representation are obvious. How meaningful is an election in which one party is guaranteed, in advance, control of the legislature (or of one of its houses) even if a substantial vote is cast against it? Yet such a result occurs in several American states with sufficient frequency to raise serious questions for a people that supposedly profess democracy as a value system.

While political parties in many states are not noted for having a high degree of internal cohesion or unity of purpose, there are often issues on which the party balance can make a decided difference. This is particularly true when the governorship is held by a popular leader who has dramatized certain matters of public policy. Yet a misrepresentative legislature (or even one house) can nullify whatever attempt is made to embody into law a program apparently endorsed by the electorate. Even a governor's choice of his own cabinet and other important appointive posts must often meet the approval of a hostile upper house.

On Intraparty Structure. In addition to affecting the two-party balance, rural dominance also plays an important role *within* each party. Legislative districts or county units commonly serve as the basis for party organizations, with a consequent advantage for rural leaders. State central committees as well as state conventions of the major parties usually reflect urban underrepresentation. The make-up of conventions is especially important in those few states where party nominees are selected by the convention method rather than the direct primary.

In some cases this imbalance within the parties has an enormous impact upon the actual selection of governing officials. For instance, party nominations for state-wide offices in Maryland are made in conventions, with delegates elected in the same manner as members of the state legislature. There is a popular election for candidates as in direct primary states, but at the convention each county or district votes as a unit. This system resembles superficially the national electoral college, though the population distortion is far less in the latter. Maryland's smallest counties, with only one-third of the state's population, send 89 of the 152 party convention delegates—or nearly three-fifths of the total. As a result there is no necessary correlation between a candidate's popular vote and his convention total. The 1950 election provided two striking examples. In the Democratic primary the incumbent governor lost in popular votes, but won the unit count and the nomination. At the same time the Republican senatorial nomination went to the candidate who had lost the popular election.

An even more publicized situation is the county-unit system of election in Georgia. Here the consequences are more far-reaching than in two-party Maryland, where opposing nominees meet in a final election in which popular votes are counted as cast. But in one-party Georgia the Democratic primary is, in effect, the only actual election. The real contests for public office are settled in the primary among party faction candidates. In place of a state-wide popular decision, every county is allotted twice the number of votes as it has representatives in the lower house of the state legislature, with each county recorded as a unit for the leading candidate within its boundaries. Since major statewide executive and judicial officers (and United States senators) are chosen by a system based on the state house of representatives, the importance of urban and rural political power in Georgia is at once obvious. With the state divided into the incredibly large number of 159 counties, representation in the lower house is allocated by the constitution according to this formula: three representatives to each of the eight most populous counties; two to each of the next thirty; and one to each of the remaining 121 counties, for a total of 205 seats. Since the 121 smallest and heavily rural counties contain only two-fifths of the state population, the inequalities are apparent. Fulton County (Atlanta) has a population of 473,572, but sends only three representatives—a delegation matched by the state's three smallest counties, with a combined population of 9,088. That Georgia politics are characterized by exceedingly rustic overtones is not surprising. The successful machine created by the late Eugene Talmadge was a natural by-product of such a pattern of power. In the 1946 gubernatorial primary Talmadge himself received 16,000 fewer popular votes than his principal opponent, but easily won the election by a score of 242 county-unit votes to 146 for his nearest rival. As a result of such an electoral arrangement, candidates make no attempt to gain a popular majority, but instead must direct their programs and appeals to the small, rural districts with the preponderant political weight.

On the Status of the County. The disproportionate weight given to local areas raises another interesting question: what is, or should be, the status of the county in the state governmental scheme? In theory and intent the county is created by the state as an administrative subdivision responsive to local needs. But as a result of the position often granted counties as representative units for the legislature, the practice in many states no longer fits the theory closely.

While county government as an administrative unit may often seem weak, the county ruling clique as a political force is unusually strong. Its lines of responsibility and accountability to the public and state are correspondingly weak. Except for a few obvious cases, such as in Georgia, the nature of county pre-eminence is unpublicized and generally goes unnoticed save by a few veteran observers. The close political ties between county officers and legislative candidates often result in a "sacred cow" position for the county. This situation is undoubtedly one of the main obstacles to much-needed reorganization of local areas. The number of counties is often far too large for an efficient utilization of services. Georgia with 159; Iowa, 99; Kentucky, 120; Illinois, 102; Missouri, 114; Kansas, 105—these are a few examples of the overextension of counties in relation to territory and population served. In many states a good share of the counties are sparsely inhabited but collectively possess a strong share of legislative power.

A thorough consolidation of smaller and weaker county units is considered by many as one of the most compelling needs in state government today. While this is generally advocated from the standpoint of administrative efficiency and economy, there could be perhaps an even more important purpose—the strengthening and revitalizing of state legislatures. One reason that modernization and reform of county services have been so slow is undoubtedly traceable to the interrelationship between county "court house rings" and state legislatures. Consolidation of counties in many states could serve as one of the most hopeful means of a more rational legislative system of representation. Yet counties, though supposedly subordinate units, often bulk so large in the actual political process that there may be little prospect for a change that could accomplish a double purpose of improved rural administration and more representative legislatures.

On Social and Economic Policies. While there are numerous determinants, both formal and informal, underlying the political process, the structural characteristics of government itself are important elements in the evolution

of public policy. Thus a legislative system based upon an unequal allocation of popular strength yields special advantages to certain interest groups
and makes the articulation of other groups more difficult. The overrepresentation of rural areas means that organized agricultural interests are usually
in a favorable position to influence state legislation. At the same time the
system places certain urban interest groups at a disadvantage. However,
those urban interests whose policies are compatible with the general outlook of rural representatives are in a more favorable position.

This fact helps explain the behavior of some urban business interests that
staunchly defend inequitable representation for their own areas. These
groups apparently find greater representation for their political outlook
among rural delegates. The alliance is not surprising in view of the frequent
similarity in attitudes held by both interests. In addition, representatives
from rural constituencies are often not farmers, but small-town lawyers and
business men. On many issues they share a natural community of interests
with city groups representing a similar social and economic outlook. By
contrast, other urban interests, notably labor groups, seldom find support
from rural representatives.

An interesting example of certain urban attitudes on representation can
be found in California, where the main supporters of the "Federal Plan"
have included the state Chamber of Commerce and its local affiliates, plus
most of the urban press. Opponents of the system have periodically sought
its repeal, the most recent attempt being a constitutional initiative campaign in 1948 aimed at modifying the degree of extreme urban underrepresentation in the senate. Main support for the initiative came from the
State Federation of Labor. The well-organized opposition was financed
primarily by interests in Los Angeles and San Francisco, both of which
areas would have gained considerably in senate representation. The Los
Angeles Chamber of Commerce, which had originally opposed an inferior
role for its own county in 1928, had in the intervening twenty years apparently been converted to the virtues of such a status. The chamber opposed
an increase from one senator to ten for Los Angeles County. Experience
with the rural-dominated senate had already shown the advantages for
conservative forces. For instance, during Democratic Governor Culbert
Olson's administration from 1939 to 1943 a "little Wagner" labor relations
act advocated by the governor passed the representative lower house in two
separate sessions, but each time died in the Republican-controlled, small-
county senate. Instances such as this undoubtedly accounted for the attitudes of both labor and business groups toward the upper house. The initiative campaign of 1948, in the face of a skillfully managed propaganda
barrage and a hostile press, lost by a wide margin, failing to carry even the
urban areas that would have increased their representative strength. To
what extent the sharp conflict of interests seen in California can be
duplicated elsewhere is difficult to determine. However, the increasingly

frequent defense by many business groups of rural overrepresentation is a general trend that cannot be ignored.

Recognition of a heterogeneous framework of interests is helpful in understanding the relative failure of labor and consumer groups to influence state legislative decisions on social and economic policy. A survey of restrictive labor legislation in a number of states reveals the leading role of rural lawmakers, often working with business approval or assistance. Other issues that have characterized distinct urban and rural conflicts include: oleomargarine taxation; educational systems; urban redevelopment and housing; liquor policies; unemployment compensation and relief; daylight saving; state planning and conservation. State legislation tends to be considerably more conservative than policies receiving public support in state-wide and national elections. Governors, whose constituencies differ (often markedly) from those of legislators, are frequently stymied in attempts to secure legislative approval for programs that have apparently been supported by a majority of the electorate. Social and economic policies endorsed by unrepresentative legislatures are undoubtedly quite different in substance or emphasis from legislation which might be expected if these bodies reflected public sentiment more accurately.

As this discussion of public policy has already indicated, inaction can be as important as positive legislative action. Some interested groups gain their objectives mainly through affirmative enactments, whereas others rely primarily on inaction and delay. The traditional American institutions of separation of powers and checks and balances, specifically devised to discourage positive government, give an immediate advantage to those groups benefiting mostly from inaction. In state legislatures a further check is usually provided by a pattern of representation that places additional obstacles in the path of interests that otherwise might influence more directly the formulation of public policy.

Some General Consequences of Unbalanced Representation. Earlier sections have suggested a number of specific consequences of unequal representation upon state government and politics. The two-party balance, intraparty structure, the status of county political power, and social and economic policies are areas most noticeably affected by rural-urban conflicts in the various states. In addition, there are a few general effects that deserve mention.

The urban-rural split in many states yields a legislature that is influenced heavily by a rural minority, but a governor more responsive to the entire state, including urban interests. While the system of separation of governmental powers inevitably invites legislative-executive friction, this is often further aggravated when each branch is accountable to different publics. Resulting stalemates tend to give a negative cast to public policy, while responsibility is diffused.

The recruitment of political leadership is also influenced by inflated rural power. In many states, opportunities for advancement within both legislature and political parties are greater for small-town politicians, especially where county-court-house rings are powerful. This is especially noticeable in the South, though it is likely to be found elsewhere to a greater extent than is generally realized.

The failure of state governments to adapt themselves to contemporary needs is a subject of increasing concern. While there are numerous reasons for the archaic institutions that characterize many states, the possibility of change or reform is often blocked by rural-urban antagonisms. Movements for much-needed constitutional conventions inevitably encounter roadblocks due to rural fears of more representative legislatures. This is probably the greatest single cause of resistance to basic constitutional change. Successful movements in the rewriting of state constitutions are usually possible only when urban areas accept a perpetuation of their subordinate role. Yet many institutional and political improvements within states await a proper urban voice in the legislature.

Finally, a less tangible matter that appears to be a partial consequence of the problem of representation is the question of public confidence in state governments. This is closely related to the ability of these governmental units to adapt themselves to the needs of contemporary society. A legislature which is able to stymie the enactment of popularly endorsed programs is hardly in a position to inspire public confidence. And, in states where rural-dominated legislatures have refused to obey constitutional mandates to reapportion, it would hardly be surprising to find a large degree of public cynicism, disillusionment, and apathy.

One important consequence that has thus far gone unmentioned now deserves consideration—the impact of state representation on city governments. As mentioned earlier, the idea of a single urban interest is unrealistic. However, there are some respects in which municipalities tend to manifest a general community of interests in the problems that affect their existence and activities. To the extent that these problems create a high degree of consensus as to the type of state policies which affect cities as governments, a separate and distinct group interest is manifested. Its status and problems form the substance of the next chapter.

The Cities Protest

Urban underrepresentation in state legislatures entails a distinct and important set of consequences for city governmental units. While every municipality faces certain unique problems, there are numerous fields of more or less common concern to city officials. Much state legislation, including vital taxation and grant-in-aid policies, bears a direct relationship to local units. The amount of flexibility allowed localities in handling their own affairs is often a source of contention as well. A sympathetic and cooperative attitude by the state is usually essential if municipalities are to give adequate attention to the increasingly complex problems of an urban and industrial society.

In actual practice, of course, cities are often handicapped by restrictive state policies. Antagonism between the states and their growing urban centers has become especially acute since the balance of population shifted to the cities, while the balance of political power remained in the rural and small town regions. An almost classic example has been the relationship of the Chicago metropolitan area vis-à-vis an Illinois legislature under downstate control. In 1925 the Cook County Board of Commissioners unanimously adopted a resolution directing the county treasurer to withhold state taxes collected by the county until the general assembly performed all its constitutional duties (meaning reapportionment). The treasurer did not comply, however. That same year the Chicago City Council adopted a resolution calling for a two-year campaign for legislative apportionment, which, if unsuccessful, was to be followed by a movement for Chicago to secede from Illinois and become a separate state. This was also a futile gesture, since the state would have to agree to a secession. But these incidents do attest to the intense city-state antagonisms that often arise from inferior urban representation.

In recent years, the United States Conference of Mayors, composed of the elected leaders of the nation's urban governments, has singled out unequal representation as the major source of trouble for municipalities in general. The organization asserts that most urban residents are virtual "second-class citizens" and are the victims of "taxation without representation." Mayors and city managers in all parts of the nation have protested the inferior status allowed municipalities in the state lawmaking bodies. Their objections are not based upon abstract theoretical principles but rather upon concrete experience. City spokesmen point specifically to discriminatory practices regarding taxation policies, state services and grants-in-aid, and state interference with local freedom of action.

Local Self-Government

While cities, like counties and other local units of government, are legally creatures of the state, they have long sought a maximum degree of autonomy and independence in the management of local problems. An example is the home-rule movement, which would allow localities to create the form of charter government and its powers best adapted to their own needs without legislative consent. Though the movement has been successful in some states, a frequent complaint of municipal officials is that home rule is either lacking or severely limited.

Often there are far too many restrictions on a city's freedom to handle purely local problems, while in many instances the details of local charters are subject to close state scrutiny. State legislatures often take up a considerable portion of their short sessions with special municipal legislation. The effect upon the more populous communities is especially noticeable. City governments often encounter specific restrictions on the use of locally collected revenues. Many state legislatures have displayed a negative attitude on such matters as city building codes, traffic safety proposals, metropolitan transportation fares, and more especially on the question of municipal annexation of adjoining unincorporated territory. Attempts by cities to cope with some of their most desperate problems are often stymied by unsympathetic legislators from small-town areas where such problems are unknown. Among states where this situation has been especially acute is Ohio. There urban redevelopment legislation, aimed at eliminating blighted slum areas, has in the past met a quick death in the lower house, where rural counties are heavily overrepresented.

Some mayors have complained that virtually any legislation sponsored by municipalities arouses an almost automatic resistance from rural legislators. Other city executives have found rural lawmakers more disinterested than hostile, except when specific urban-rural interests clashed. "Representatives of rural areas," Mayor Frank Zeidler has contended, "either fail to understand city problems or are suspicious of the motives of Milwaukee and other urban areas." Whether the friction is caused by a lack of understanding and interest or by outright hostility, the fact remains that rural legislators often wield a powerful influence upon municipal problems with which they do not have an intimate acquaintance.

Local Tax Problems

An increasingly critical situation for municipalities over the past several years is the financial structure of local governments. While local taxation has shown consistent increases, it has been unable to keep pace with the enormous disbursements needed. Municipal expenditures nationally have exceeded revenues every year since the end of World War II, with resulting increases in outstanding indebtedness.

The main reasons for the ever-tightening squeeze on the city purse are to be found in the huge construction needs for schools and roads. The sharp rise in birth rates during and after World War II, together with a wartime suspension of construction, accounted for an unanticipated demand for new classroom space. Also, many communities whose former growth patterns had been stable were confronted with a sizeable influx of new inhabitants and a resulting demand for an immediate expansion of city services and facilities.

While state governments have also had their share of post-war financial headaches, they are in a more favorable position regarding revenues than are municipalities. The state can tax a large variety of sources—income, sales, excises, property, and others. Municipalities, however, are limited to those sources which the state allows them to tap. The property tax, unsatisfactory from a number of standpoints, has remained the producer of the great bulk of local revenue. In order to meet pressing new fiscal needs, cities have sought—sometimes with success—to enter additional revenue-producing fields. In general, however, states allow localities far too little authority to remedy their financial difficulties.

State legislative approval is often required before city officials can work out annual taxation and budget policies. If the legislature contained a proportionate number of urban representatives, the local picture would be more fully comprehended. Instead, municipal spokesmen must usually present their cases to representatives from rural areas without problems of a comparable magnitude. Late in 1953 the mayor of St. Louis found it necessary to schedule an 1,800-mile journey through Missouri's hinterlands to talk to rural legislators. His mission was to gain an extension of his city's earnings tax beyond its scheduled expiration date.

Municipal executives have pointed to a number of specific state tax policies that discriminate against urban areas. A frequent complaint centers around the distribution of highway funds from gasoline and auto license fees. Street and highway construction and maintenance constitute (next to education) the second largest item in municipal budgets. Here also, cities have felt the impact of unusually extensive programs of repair and rehabilitation necessitated by wartime inaction. But many legislatures have turned deaf ears to municipal appeals for help and cooperation. For several years the League of Texas Municipalities has been unsuccessfully pleading that cities receive a share of the state gasoline tax. One Texas city manager has contended that 65 per cent of this state tax is paid by urban residents whose travel mileage is 90 per cent within the corporate limits of the larger cities. Yet the state allows no part of the tax to help supplement hard-pressed municipal budgets for street repair. When cities do share in the distribution of state auto license and gasoline taxes, their proportion usually suffers by comparison with rural districts. For instance, the formula in Iowa was recently reported to be: 42 per cent to state highways; 35 per cent for county secondary roads (allocated on the basis of county area); 15 per cent for farm-to-market roads; and 8 per cent to cities.

A like discrimination is often charged regarding state distribution of its sales tax revenues. For example, Ohio's sales tax receipts were originally allocated on a formula of 40 per cent to local governments (on a tax duplicate basis) and 60 per cent to public schools. However, small counties, with a strong voice in the legislature, managed to whittle down the formula with the insertion of a minimum distribution to each county. As a result, the share going to Ohio's cities was reduced to little more than one third of its original amount.

Other sources of unrest on tax policies include: unequalized assessments on rural and urban property; inequitable county tax structures; and financial burdens imposed on cities by services they must render to suburban areas.

State Services and Grants-in-Aid

Due to their expanding responsibilities as well as superior revenue sources, state governments have been rendering an increasing amount of assistance to local units for matters of state-wide importance. The rapid rise over the past several years of grants-in-aid to subordinate levels of government signifies an important attempt to provide a more uniform approach to certain services (notably education, welfare, and roads) while at the same time helping to equalize the financial burdens of localities that vary in tax-producing wealth.

While state services and grants have eased the problems of many local units, the basis of distribution is a subject of widespread controversy. Frequent complaints are heard from city officials to the effect that state aid for education and highways greatly favors rural over urban areas, with no proper relationship to need. One reason is that the distribution of state funds is often based on the assessed valuation of local property, with the assumption that lower assessments indicate greater need. However, rural property is often grossly undervalued by local assessors, who fear for re-election. Urban assessments are generally far closer to true value.

To the extent that urban communities are more prosperous, a lesser degree of state aid is justifiable. It is often assumed that cities are inevitably wealthier than rural areas. Yet such a condition is far from uniform. Many rural and suburban localities are in a stronger financial condition than cities, yet receive substantially more state aid.

In some instances, municipalities suffer from a double squeeze—the state greatly restricts their taxing powers and at the same time renders little assistance in the form of grants-in-aid or shared revenues. A good example is Connecticut, which in 1948 ranked fourth among states in per capita individual income, but stood 41st in the amount of aid per capita to local governments. At the same time, Connecticut's cities are restricted to the property tax for nearly all local revenue. Of the state's financial aid that is distributed, rural areas benefit far more than do cities. Connecticut's state education grants have been allocated solely on the basis of total numbers of pupils in average daily attendance, with the amount per pupil declining drastically for units with larger enrollments. A recent report indicated that Hartford's annual share averaged $31 per student as compared with up to $110 per pupil in small communities. State highway grants also have been designed so that small communities reap far greater benefits. According to city spokesmen, some small Connecticut towns have occasionally found it unnecessary to levy a local property tax, since state aids covered their requirements completely.

Alternatives for Cities

Failing to get a proper voice in the state legislature, municipalities have been forced to seek alternative ways of gaining some recognition of the vast problems confronting them. One natural locus of influence is the state's executive branch, which is more subject to urban voting power than are most legislatures. As a result, the governor and other state administrative officials can often be expected to lend more sympathetic ears to urban complaints and proposals. When the governor himself supports the city point of view he may be able to use his powers so as to alleviate some urban problems. In many instances, however (especially in rural states), there is little difference between the outlook of executives and legislators. Partisan considerations also account for many variations. In any case, a sympathetic executive, however helpful, is hardly a substitute for equal legislative strength.

Another route circumventing rural-dominated state legislatures has been that of direct relationships between cities and agencies of the federal government. Over the past two decades especially, federal-municipal ties have developed in a number of important fields. Mayor Charles Henderson of Youngstown, Ohio, has suggested that there is a direct connection between a rural-oriented and unsympathetic state legislature and the necessity for municipal-federal relations. The mayor specified: "In old age pensions, assistance to hospitals and aid to the local health departments the federal government has aided cities where the state had failed. This is a bad and dangerous tendency, but one brought about entirely by the slowness of the state of Ohio."

A final approach that has proved useful is the growing degree of co-operation among cities within a state in seeking action on matters of common concern. Leagues of municipalities do effective work in many states, especially in helping eliminate jealousies and rivalry between large and small cities. The result is often a more unified presentation of urban proposals. In the absence of equal representation in legislatures, municipal cooperation may prove to be a significant force in surmounting at least some adverse effects on cities of rural dominance.

The foregoing paragraphs have sketched a few of the principal consequences of unbalanced representation upon cities as operating units of government. Clearer insights concerning the impact of state policies in action can be gained by a closer examination of a specific controversy between a city and state. For this reason the next section is devoted to a brief case study of the financial dispute involving New York City and the state government during the winter and spring of 1954. Details of this dramatic clash of interests may help illustrate some of the ramifications— both economic and political—involved in the relationship of metropolis to state.

New York City: A Case Study

Sectional political conflict in New York State cannot acurately be described as urban versus rural in the usual sense. Rather, the real issue is generally New York City versus the rest of the state. Upstate areas contain a number of large municipalities, but most of them are usually politically allied with rural areas against the metropolitan center.

Fear and jealousy of the big city by the rest of the state have resulted in an inferior status for New York City in both houses of the legislature. Generations ago, shrewd and farsighted upstate politicians, aware of the city's potential growth, made sure that it would never elect a majority of the legislature, regardless of its population. The state constitution of 1894 placed virtually permanent control of both houses in the upstate region. The lower house membership was fixed at 150, with at least one member guaranteed to each of the state's 62 counties (except for two which are combined for representative purposes). The constitution calls for senate districts to contain, as nearly as may be, an equal number of inhabitants (excluding aliens). Yet this goal is made impossible by a contradictory and complicated provision that the senate be enlarged proportionately whenever large counties merit more than three senators each, as determined by a formula.

As a result, New York City has been denied a proportionate share of legislative strength. With approximately 53 per cent of the state's population, the city elects 43.3 per cent of the assembly and 43.1 per cent of the senate. The sharp rural bias is shown by the fact that the state's 22 smallest county-districts, with a total population of 749,295, send 22 assemblymen to Albany—the same total as New York City's largest county, Kings, with a population of 2,738,175.

One of the most noticeable effects of metropolitan underrepresentation in New York pertains to the major party balance. Since the city is strongly Democratic and the rest of the state is heavily Republican, it takes a landslide of almost miracle proportions to remove the GOP from control of both houses. In modern times this has happened only once—in 1934. Republican-directed reapportionments since then make a repetition of such an occurrence in the future highly remote. The state legislature promises to serve as a Republican bulwark even in solidly Democratic areas.

In view of this background, political tensions in New York between the state government and the large metropolis are understandable. The fact that the party split also reflects the sectional antagonism tends to re-emphasize the divergent points of view. One basic issue that has proven especially controversial for several years is the financial relationship between the city and the state. The fight which had long simmered broke into a raging boil during the winter and spring of 1954.

City-State Financial Friction. Since the end of World War II particularly, city-state frictions have intensified. The financial problems of both levels of government are closely interrelated. The state derives the largest part of its revenues from the people and business life of New York City. On the other hand, the city can claim for its own needs only those taxing powers permitted it by the state. Further aggravating the relationship has been the state's insistence that grants of taxing power to the city be short-term. As a result, city officials must make annual trips to Albany before they can determine revenue sources for a city budget that exceeds the entire state budget by more than half a billion dollars.

The stage was set for a battle royal with the approach of the mayoralty election for New York City in November 1953. The Democratic candidate, Robert F. Wagner, ran on a platform that included the goal of new city-state fiscal arrangements and an end to a subservient "hat-in-hand" attitude by the city in its dealings with Albany. Candidate Wagner saw a direct connection between the city's financial plight and her legislative strength. He predicted that "New York City is going to be short-changed by Albany just so long as we are under-represented in a Republican-controlled Legislature."[2] He further called upon Governor Dewey to present a resolution for an amendment to the state constitution in order to eliminate the city's unequal representative status. Metropolitan Democrats were still smarting from a Republican legislative reapportionment early in the year. The measure reduced New York City's already inferior strength in each house and in addition drew district lines so as to minimize Democratic strength still further.

With Wagner's election by a substantial margin in November 1953, the lines of battle were clearly drawn. Since the new city administration's first major task would be to draw up a budget for the next fiscal year, plans and proposals began to evolve of necessity even before the new mayor's inaugural. It was clear that any program would lay stress on two areas—greater state aid and expanded local taxing powers.

Of special concern to city forces was legislative curtailment of the local property tax, the only source of city revenue guaranteed by the state constitution. A recent amendment, approved by the electorate, increased the limit upon the real estate tax from two to two and one-half per cent. However, the legislature had limited the city to only one half of the allowable increase. Even this partial rise was made contingent upon the city's turning over municipal transportation lines to a Transit Authority. In order to foil any possible attempt by the city to circumvent the transit transfer, the legislature also placed sharp limits on the city's power to issue special bonds or budget notes. City spokesmen considered such legislation "punitive" and called for its repeal now that a Transit Authority had been established.

The question of state aid had also become increasingly controversial. An average of approximately 55 per cent of state revenues is derived from New York City. Yet the city's share of state aid had dropped to less than 45 per cent. Since the state allocates approximately 55 per cent of its revenues to local governments, this is a substantial source for local budgets. While New York City had received back from the state less than it had contributed for several decades, the disparity has grown wider in recent years. This can be shown by the following chart:

(All figures indicate percentage of state total)

Year	New York City Population	State Revenues from New York City	State Aid to New York City
1930	55.0	61.8	52.1
1940	55.3	55.5	48.8
1953	53.2	55.3	44.8

The difference between population and city revenue-yield to the state in 1930 indicates greater tax-producing wealth and a higher per capita contribution than in other areas of the state. This would account for some of the disparity between city contribution and state aid in that year. Democrats contended that the city's interests were partially protected from a hostile legislature when their party held the governor's office (as in both 1930 and 1940). The decrease in the city's share of state aid since 1942 they attributed to Republican control of both legislative and executive branches.

Lines of Battle, 1954. Shortly before taking office, Mayor-elect Wagner and his fiscal advisers had evolved a set of proposals that would give the city additional revenues of $145,000,000. The major points in the program were:

1. New York City should be allowed taxing powers without time limits.

2. Certain irrevocable and exclusive taxing powers should be given to the city.

3. The legislature should restore to the city full use of the constitutionally authorized tax of 2.5 per cent on real estate. This would produce some $50,000,000 for the city and still leave its tax rate the lowest of the state's sixty-two cities.

4. The state should turn over to the city state income tax payments of non-residents, 90 per cent of whom commute from Connecticut and New Jersey to New York City. The city rather than the state must bear the cost of providing services for them. This would bring an additional $20,000,000 in city revenue.

5. New York City should receive equal treatment with the state's other localities in the distribution of state aid and shared taxes.

The all-important proposals regarding increased state aid fell into three main categories. First, the city pointed out that the state's other fifty-seven counties (but not New York City's five) receive from the state one fourth of the motor vehicle license fees and 10 per cent of the state gasoline tax collected within their borders. A similar allocation to the metropolitan area was requested. Second, the new administration asserted that the city had approximately 42 per cent of the public school population of the state, but received only 31 per cent of total state aid to education. For each New York City pupil the state contributed $95 compared to $155 for each child enrolled outside the city. Finally, the proposal was made that the state university system assume operation of the four municipal colleges in New York City. In order to lessen the impact upon state financial policies, the mayor-elect suggested that the proposed shifts in state aid take place gradually over a four year period.

These new proposals were spelled out in a detailed letter from Mayor-elect Wagner to Governor Dewey. Within twenty-four hours the governor summarily rejected the requests for greater state aid as "obviously advanced in bad faith." The local tax proposals would be reserved for further study. Later the governor and his fiscal advisers asserted that New York City received proportionately less state aid because it contained a larger proportionate volume of taxable wealth and was thus in less need of state assistance. City spokesmen answered that this situation was no longer true. They further contended that the state measured local taxable wealth on the basis of real estate assessments. This they felt was unreliable in view of the deliberate underassessment of property in many upstate localities. Support for this view was indicated in a fresh survey by the State Board of Equalization and Assessment, showing that some upstate assessments were "shockingly" below value.

In February 1954, Mayor Wagner and his advisers journeyed to Albany to discuss the fiscal situation with the governor and his staff. The New York *Times* report of the meeting seemed to suggest a symbolic significance in the locale: "The conference took place not in Governor Dewey's private office, but in the huge, red-carpeted executive chamber, which is used principally for clemency hearings for convicted felons."[3] It is safe to say that the meeting produced no significant changes in the attitude of either side. Indeed, the governor had already sent his new budget to the legislature and refused to consider any deviations in the state aid provisions. Of the approximately $614,000,000 in financial assistance to local governments, about $257,000,000 was allocated to New York City. All Democratic attempts in the legislature to amend the budget were foredoomed to failure.

The controversy continued unabated throughout the spring. Both the mayor and governor took their cases to the radio and television audiences on several occasions. The state controller issued reports in support of the Republican administration's position. These were immediately countered by reports from the city's budget director defending the mayor's program. The main argument used by the state was: New York City is not discriminated against, but has more than doubled its total amount of state aid since 1941. The city answered that measuring the increase in total amounts was misleading, since aid to all localities had increased greatly, with proportionate gains by other areas being substantially greater than those of New York City. Since 1941 aid to the city showed an increase of about 110 per cent, as compared to 180 per cent for the rest of the state.

While Mayor Wagner's administration had probably never been really optimistic about gaining substantial changes in state assistance, it had apparently held some hope for greater local taxing powers, since these would not affect state policy. But even here the state budged only partially. On the largest item—lifting the limit on realty assessments—the state finally authorized the city to go beyond the former rate of 2¼ per cent only to the extent of $38,000,000 instead of the $50,000,000 that would be gained from the full constitutional maximum.

The City Loses. With its program largely rejected by the state, the city administration announced it was forced to drop former plans for salary increases to its employees and teachers. It would also have to retain certain "nuisance" taxes, such as a special auto fee. But the new budget still showed a gap of some $30,000,000 between potential revenue and planned expenditures. The city council and mayor made several unsuccessful appeals for a special legislative session to grant additional taxing powers. The state insisted that the potential deficit be made up in two ways: by budgeting certain reserve funds; and by levying certain taxes that the city had authority for using. The city answered that the first step would be financially foolhardy and possibly illegal; the city also rejected what it considered as state attempts to impose "obnoxious" nuisance taxes while placing political responsibility for them on the city government.

The city council finally evolved a budget by imposing a 5 per cent tax on amusements. This aroused protests from the city's large amusement trade, just as alternative proposals had met opposition from other groups which would have been affected. The city government, while expressing regret at the new levy, considered it the least "obnoxious" of the alternatives available. The city further placed the entire responsibility on the state's intransigent attitude.

As early as January 1954, Mayor Wagner proposed the creation of an impartial commission to study the fiscal relations between city and state, with an equal number of members appointed by both the mayor and the governor. The suggestion was repeated several times throughout the year and was echoed by a resolution of the city council. On each occasion the proposal was immediately scorned by both the governor and Republican legislators. Governor Dewey termed the suggestion "arrogant and presumptuous" and charged that Mayor Wagner was attempting to dictate the state's fiscal policies. The state administration also pointed out that a Temporary State Commission on Fiscal Affairs had long been studying the entire financial picture of the state, which would include the question of state-local relationships. In reply, city officials observed that the commission already in operation consisted of persons named only by Governer Dewey and the legislature, with Republicans predominating. They felt that such a group could not be sufficiently impartial in regard to the city's fiscal problems.

Partisan overtones were evident from the start of the controversy. The Democrats were more united than they had been in years, with party leadership in Albany giving support from the start to the new mayor's program. The overwhelmingly Democratic city council naturally backed the proposals. Republicans were similarly unified in supporting the governor's stand. Even GOP legislators from New York City, plus the two Republicans on the city council, opposed the Wagner approach. With important state elections forthcoming in November 1954, neither party lost an opportunity to make political capital. During the gubernatorial campaign, Mayor Wagner advised his constituents that only the election of Democratic candidate Averell Harriman would ease the city's troubles. Conversely, Republican candidate Irving Ives warned upstate residents that a shift to a Democratic governor would work only to the interests of New York City. The election of Mr. Harriman promised at least an abatement of the conflict between Albany and Gotham. Since the legislature naturally remained in Republican control, some stalemate on state policy appeared inevitable, though the city's bargaining power would doubtless be strengthened by a Democratic executive.

An Evaluation. In spite of the partisanship surrounding much of the controversy, it seems possible to suggest certain conclusions that can stand quite apart from the party battle involved. In the first place, it appears clear beyond any question that New York City's entire status in respect to the state is unsatisfactory. There can be no reasonable justification for a situation in which officials of the nation's largest metropolis are forced constantly to seek the approval of a distant and often hostile state government for detailed revenue items in the city's annual budget. The paternalistic attitude adopted by unsympathetic state officials can hardly encourage a spirit of local responsibility in determining local needs. It is doubtful if perpetual crises can be avoided without more flexible and stable powers being allocated to the city.

Second, the specific action of the legislature in restricting the city's use of the property tax to an amount that the state feels the city needs is difficult to defend. The electorate had approved a constitutional increase in the maximum tax and city officials were willing to assume the political responsibility. In such a situation legislative interference is a disrupting element.

Third, while both state and city officials deplored the "playing of politics" by the other camp, such a game by both sides is inevitable so long as the city's fiscal affairs are so directly dependent upon state approval. New York mayoralty candidates run on platforms which they are almost powerless to implement if the state government is held by the other party. Republican state leaders are unwilling to give specific assistance in making a Democratic city administration look good. On the contrary they are in a position to force city officials into making financial decisions that may be politically unpopular. As a consequence the Democrats feel that the only solution is to win the governor's office. Thus both parties take the fiscal picture into the pre-election headlines.

Finally, the city's charge that it receives an unfairly small share of state financial aid involves too complex a picture for a ready conclusion. While much of Mayor Wagner's bill of particulars seems valid on its face, and while much of the state's rebuttal was vague and inconclusive, the whole question of a "fair" allocation of state funds is sufficiently complicated to require further study. Consequently, the proposals by New York City spokesmen for a study commission seem entirely reasonable. Governor Dewey's consistent refusal to consider such a step leaves the impression, rightly or wrongly, that the state administration is not too confident of its position. The commission already engaged in a more comprehensive review of the state's financial condition may help resolve some of the issues involved in state-local assistance. Yet, the city's reluctance to accept findings of a Republican-appointed group is understandable. The conclusions and recommendations of an expert commission, with members named by both city and state governments, would carry more weight.

Any long-range solution to New York City's problems appears dependent upon its gaining a truly representative voice in the state lawmaking body. The existing pattern of representation only intensifies the antagonism and distrust. It is hardly surprising that New York City taxpayers, outvoted in Albany regardless of their numbers, are frustrated and confused.

This case study of New York's financial difficulties is not presented as a necessarily "typical" instance of urban-rural antagonism, since no single pattern would be applicable throughout the country. Seldom, in fact, are urban-rural issues so sharply delineated and dramatically publicized as in the case of New York. There are a number of unique features that help explain this.

For one thing, New York is the only city in the United States whose inhabitants comprise a clear majority of the state population. A bipolarization of feeling is thus intensified. The remainder of the state, including several sizeable municipalities, has shown a traditional suspicion of Gotham, thus reducing the possibilities of municipal unity vis-à-vis the legislature.

In addition, the degree of strength and discipline shown by the two political parties is not duplicated in many other states. The widespread publicity over the 1954 budget fight was due partially to maneuvering by both parties in order to obtain public support for their particular stands. Elsewhere, existing urban-legislative antagonisms are often obscured by such factors as weak state parties and nonpartisan municipal elections.

Yet, in spite of some features unique to New York City, the controversy there also presents in unusually clear focus a number of problems that are fairly common to other cities. Restricted taxing powers and insufficient grants-in-aid are especially worth noting here. Rural advantage through unusually low property assessment seems another feature that is common to many states. And elsewhere, as in New York City, municipal executives often place a large measure of blame on the inadequate representation allowed the city in the state legislature.

While equal representation is no panacea for all urban problems, it can at least clarify the question of responsibility and provide a sounder psychological climate for political institutions.

Unbalanced Representation at the National Level

Rural versus urban patterns of political power constitute an important facet of national as well as state and local politics. The nature of the problem is somewhat different, but much of it reflects a direct impact of the situation already noticed in the states.

The United States Senate and Urbanism

It has been traditional to consider the equal representation of states in the United States Senate as the chief national manifestation of over-represented rural power. Indeed, the distortions from the ideal of "one man, one vote" are greater in the national upper house than in many state legislatures. The constitutional compromise of 1787, arrived at when the union was a far looser federation than it later became, has vested tremendous power in thinly populated areas. Today the ten most populous states contain over half of the nation's inhabitants, but have only twenty senators to the seventy-six of the remaining states.

The result of this disproportionate representation in the American federal system has been to give an advantage to economic interests located in the less populous states. Historically these interests have been mainly agricultural. The most striking example is an entire region of thinly populated states, the Rocky Mountain area. The disproportionate influence of senators from that region has frequently been noticeable in legislation affecting economic activities common to much of the region. Silver mining and sugar beet interests have often received preferential national attention. If one regards only effective voting population, the South is another region that historically has been overrepresented in the Senate, and Southern interests have often benefited. It is a rare piece of protective farm legislation that does not include cotton, peanuts, rice, and tobacco among the most "basic" crops.

Despite the disparity in the size of Senate constituencies, the traditional view that the result is rural overrepresentation may have to be modified for two reasons. One is that the degree of urbanism has become sufficiently widespread so that the number of preponderantly rural states is rapidly declining. According to the classification of the 1950 United States census, thirty of the forty-eight states are more urban than rural, with twenty of these claiming 60 per cent or more of their population as urban. The second reason is the fact that a state's two senators are elected at large and must appeal to as many significant interests within the state as possible. Even many rural states have a substantial urban populace that cannot be ignored. Thus most senators can be expected to be actively aware of urban interests and problems.

The House of "Misrepresentatives"

Ironically, a good case can be made for the proposition that the Senate is more representative in respect to urban and rural political power than the lower house of Congress, supposedly based on a general population standard. Due partly to the impact of unrepresentative state legislatures on the make-up of congressional districts, the lower house has become more a House of "Misrepresentatives."

Apportionment of Congressional Districts. Since the Senate represents political units rather than people, it is all the more essential that the lower house of Congress be faithfully designed to reflect population. Indeed, nearly all members of the constitutional convention of 1787 which accepted a compromise Senate were agreed that the House of Representatives must be the "grand depository of the democratic principle."[2] As a result the Constitution stipulated that representatives "shall be apportioned among the several States . . . according to their respective Numbers . . ." (with a minimum of one for each state). The manner of electing the various representatives within each state is left to the respective legislatures, subject to ultimate congressional control. One reason for empowering Congress to alter state regulations or to make new ones is of more than historic interest. James Madison explained apprehensions that "the inequality of the representation in the legislatures of particular states would produce a like inequality in their representation in the national legislature, as it was presumable that the counties having the power in the former case would secure it to themselves in the latter."[3]

Decennial apportionment statutes passed by Congress over the latter part of the nineteenth century attempted to set standards for states to follow that would assure fair districting. Eventually states were supposed to create congressional districts of compact and contiguous territory and containing "as nearly as practicable" equal numbers of inhabitants. In 1929 Congress adopted an "automatic" reapportionment statute that empowers the President, in the absence of new legislation, to allot the proper number of congressional seats among the states after each census. However, the former safeguards for fair districting within states were omitted.

When President Truman in 1951 announced the new apportionment of representatives as a result of population changes revealed by the 1950 census, he asked Congress to reinstate the former statutory requirement of equal single-member districts, and to require in addition a maximum percentage deviation allowable within any state. Both the President and the reapportionment committee of the American Political Science Association suggested that approximately a 15 per cent deviation both above and below the average district population gives sufficient flexibility to the states. This would allow districts to vary over a range from about 300,000 to 400,000 people based on the 1950 census. Representative Emanuel Celler of New York introduced a bill which would establish this standard with enforcement provisions, and which would also restore the requirements of compactness and contiguity. However, Congress showed little enthusiasm for the proposal.

In the current absence of federal regulations, state legislatures are free to do about as they please on the matter of redistricting congressional seats. The implications of this power, combined with the unrepresentative nature of most state legislatures, lead to results that are hardly surprising. State lawmakers have been almost as cavalier about periodic equalization of congressional districts as they have been about reapportioning their own seats. The only sanction of any consequence which forces some states to act is a change in their total share of House membership. When a state loses congressional strength it must either redistrict or elect all representatives at large. Since the latter eventuality is usually feared by politicians of both parties, some type of redistricting ordinarily results. If a state gains membership, only the additional seat or seats are elected at large in the event of legislative failure to act. This alternative is often chosen when disagreement over districting arises.

Present Inequalities among Congressional Districts.   As a result of significant nation-wide population shifts between 1940 and 1950, nine states lost representatives, while seven gained new ones. Consequently, redistricting has taken place in several states since 1951. The results of the process, however, have generally not met equitable standards. And since cities are already underrepresented in the very agency responsible for setting up congressional districts, their consequent inferior status in the national House of Representatives is not surprising. Table 3 lists all states that have redistricted between 1951 and 1954, with the largest and smallest district populations given to indicate the most extreme distortions. Urban districts are noted where they occur.

Since the national average population for each congressman should be 344,846 (though the average varies somewhat from state to state) the numerous deviations from the standard are apparent from a glance at

Table 3. With only a few exceptions the largest and hence most under-represented areas are urban. In the cases of Chicago and Los Angeles it should be noted that the cities receive their proper number of total seats. Distortions of constituencies within the cities probably result from gerrymandering. The only states that kept close to the advocated 15 per cent deviation limit were New York and Virginia. Three of the states in Table 3 neither gained nor lost total congressional membership. Of these, redistricting in West Virginia and New Jersey made only minor changes in the over-all pattern. The third, Ohio, did not succeed in avoiding some gross disparities in district strength.

TABLE 3

Congressional Redistricting, 1951–1954

Selected Districts	Populations	Selected Districts	Populations
ARKANSAS		**NEW JERSEY**	
1 (Little Rock)	407,480	1 (Camden)	441,978
2	224,278	2	258,127
CALIFORNIA		**NEW YORK**	
26 (Los Angeles)	480,827	37	393,130
22 (Los Angeles)	219,018	43	297,131
FLORIDA		**OHIO**	
4 (Miami)	525,051	3 (Dayton)	545,644
8	210,428	12 (Columbus)	503,410
ILLINOIS		15	226,341
13 (Chicago)	466,064	**OKLAHOMA**	
20	281,468	1 (Tulsa)	439,518
KENTUCKY		5 (Oklahoma City)	436,620
3 (Louisville)	484,615	3	266,995
1	304,978	**PENNSYLVANIA**	
MARYLAND		26	444,921
5 (suburban)	426,371	14 (Reading)	255,740
1	210,623	**TENNESSEE**	
MICHIGAN		9 (Memphis)	482,393
16 (Detroit, Dearborn)	525,334	7	247,912
6 (Flint, Lansing)	470,629	**VIRGINIA**	
14 (Detroit)	466,448	2 (Norfolk, Portsmouth)	403,923
12	178,251	7	289,498
MISSISSIPPI		**WEST VIRGINIA**	
4 (Jackson, Vicksburg)	426,396	6 (Charleston)	446,466
2	281,287	1	279,954
MISSOURI			
1 (St. Louis)	427,856		
3 (St. Louis)	426,088		
8	276,499		

As might be expected, it is in states that take no redistricting action after each census where the greatest inequalities occur. Here there is no pressure to form new districts as there is in states losing or gaining congressmen. The result again is underrepresentation of cities in the House of Representatives due to inaction by rotten borough state legislatures. Table 4 lists some of the typical distortions found, with urban centers again noted. Date of last redistricting is also included in parentheses.

TABLE 4

Outdated Districting

Selected Districts	*Populations*	*Selected Districts*	*Populations*
ALABAMA (1931)		**MINNESOTA (1933)**	
9 (Birmingham)	558,928	3 (Minneapolis)	433,942
6	250,726	9	273,125
CONNECTICUT (1931)		**OREGON (1941)**	
1 (Hartford)	539,661	3 (Portland)	468,571
4 (Bridgeport)	504,342	1	432,448
5	274,300	2	245,976
(1 Congressman at large)		**TEXAS (1933)**	
GEORGIA (1931)		8 (Houston)	806,701
5 (Atlanta)	618,431	5 (Dallas)	614,799
9	246,227	20 (San Antonio)	500,460
INDIANA (1941)		17	226,739
11 (Indianapolis)	551,777	(1 Congressman at large)	
9	258,441	**WASHINGTON (1931)**	
IOWA (1941)		1 (Seattle)	527,768
2 (Des Moines)	414,421	6 (Tacoma)	456,653
4	252,926	3	321,162
KANSAS (1941)		(1 Congressman at large)	
4 (Wichita)	448,435	**WISCONSIN (1931)**	
3	227,270	4 (Milwaukee)	438,041
LOUISIANA (1912)		5 (Milwaukee)	433,006
6 (Baton Rouge)	417,898	10	249,654
8	249,776		

From a national standpoint the situation revealed by both action and inaction of state legislatures on congressional redistricting adds up to a considerable over-all dilution of city strength in the House of Representatives. For instance, the nation's thirteen largest districts, all of them urban and each containing over 500,000 inhabitants, total enough population collectively for approximately twenty-two congressmen instead of thirteen. It is likely that a computation of all large city districts in the nation would show a shortage of at least two dozen seats.

This situation can be traced to a number of causes. Attempts to protect the positions of incumbent representatives, plus partisan, sectional, and personal antagonisms all play a part in the outcome. Yet the fact that the largest and most underrepresented districts are nearly always urban, while the smallest ones are generally rural, would seem to indicate more than merely an interesting coincidence on a nation-wide scale. The resulting congressional pattern is obviously a partial reflection of state legislative and political institutions wholly unrepresentative of their own citizens.

Gerrymandering. An additional feature of importance is gerrymandering. In some cases this involves a distortion in district populations. However, it is entirely possible for a state to be divided equitably population-wise, but with the lines so drawn to benefit the party in control of the state legislature. For instance, Massachusetts is notorious for its Republican-rigged congressional map, even though district populations are relatively equal. Another good example is New York's 1952 redistricting act, by which the Republican legislature found it simple to gerrymander without unduly distorting district populations. The new twelfth district twists and turns through the center of heavily Democratic Brooklyn to include enough Republican strength for an extra seat. The resulting configuration bears a striking resemblance to the original Gerrymander of 1812. Democratic Oklahoma has managed to corral most Republican strength in the state into an odd-shaped district that includes several northern rural counties before jutting down to take in barely adjoining Tulsa County.

In some states the majority party allocates the proper number of congressional seats to large cities, but then proceeds to underrepresent the opposing party in the drawing of boundaries. California furnishes an excellent example. There the Republican legislature in 1951 produced a remarkably effective gerrymander of Los Angeles County. Of the county's twelve congressional seats, three were created with populations close to a theoretical average. The remaining districts were grossly over- or underpopulated. While considerable disparities are unfortunately inevitable due to certain state constitutional requirements on the composition of districts, all of the resulting distortions in Los Angeles County happened to benefit the Republican Party. This is seen by placing the nine over- and underpopulated districts into two groups:

Overrepresented		Underrepresented	
District	*Population*	*District*	*Population*
16	223,703	17	431,254
18	286,505	19	453,942
20	226,679	23	421,623
22	219,018	26	480,827
24	287,325		
Totals:	1,243,230		1,787,646

All of the overrepresented districts in the left column proved to be Republican in the 1952 congressional election, while all of the under-represented ones turned out to be Democratic. This "coincidence" meant that the four Democratic representatives stood for nearly half again as many people as the five Republican representatives. The county's remaining three average-sized districts were Republican. Thus in a county where the two parties were almost evenly balanced in voting strength (Republican candidates took 52 per cent of the total congressional votes in 1952), Democrats could claim only four of the twelve seats in the House of Representatives. This type of gerrymandering within city districts is common in many other states. The result is that certain urban interests receive less influence than they might otherwise expect, while other urban groups can gain an undue advantage.

The process of drawing district lines so as to minimize the opposing party's strength is often accepted as standard ground rules in American politics. Indeed, many state legislatures proceed to redistrict on the assumption that they have some sort of a popular mandate directing the victor to monopolize the spoils. Sometimes partisan leaders display a bold frankness in admitting and even boasting of gerrymandering. From a Missouri Democrat came this reply to Republican protests over the 1952 congressional districting there:

Did the Republicans really expect the Democrats to draft and support a redistricting bill favorable to the Republicans? If they did their political training has been sadly neglected and their political acumen hovers near the zero mark. The Republicans are entitled to the same redistricting feast at the hands of the Democrats that they would serve the Democrats if they were in power. Only that—and nothing more.[4]

In a similar vein is the justification of the recent Republican gerrymander of New York's forty-three districts. Senate majority leader Arthur Wicks said candidly:

It would be hypocritical for me to deny that the bill may bring about an increased Republican representation in Congress. Of course, that is to be expected of legislation enacted by a Legislature which is controlled by the Republicans because the people of the state voted more Republicans than Democrats into the Legislature.[5]

These statements, though unusually frank, are fairly typical examples of the attitudes held by majority parties in state legislatures. Gerrymandering becomes justified on the professed assumption that the "people" freely elected a legislature controlled by one party. Yet the unequal strength which the "people" are allowed in most state legislatures goes unmentioned. Even where the majority party does represent a true majority of the public, there are serious objections to allowing congressional redistricting to be treated like a political plum. More than local partisan and sectional interests are involved in the result, since the whole fabric of national lawmaking is at issue.

While there is no "qualitative" difference between a Democratic gerrymander in one state and a Republican gerrymander in another, there is a quantitative difference. Outside the South, most state legislatures are regularly in Republican hands, in many cases only because of unbalanced representation. In most areas of the South the Democrats are so thoroughly entrenched that there is no minority party voting strength of sufficient consequence to gerrymander. The result is that in close national elections the composition of constituency boundaries gives the Republicans an initial advantage in the battle for congressional seats (outside the South). In Southern states districting generally works to the advantage of the more conservative, rural-based factions within the Democratic Party.

There is a compelling need to remove the districting function from any party monopoly in the various states, and especially where the controlling party is unrepresentative. While the elimination of all partisan inequities cannot be expected, there is surely room for tremendous improvement. At the very least, Congress should enact legislation embodying proposals such as those initiated by Representative Celler. Some have suggested going a step farther and transferring the entire districting function from state legislatures to a national bipartisan commission of eminent citizens. Such a group has been charged with similar responsibilities in Great Britain, though it seems unlikely that a United States Congress with such strong local ties would ever approve a similar experiment here.

Rural Power in the National Government

The mere numerical advantage held by rural districts in Congress, while substantial, is minor compared with the strategic advantages they enjoy in the actual power structure of each house. Public policy is less influenced by aggregate numbers than by strategically placed congressmen who wield power far out of proportion to the size of the constituencies they represent. The more powerful congressional committees usually reflect a disproportionate rural membership. Further, the most influential members, the committee chairmen, rise to their positions solely by virtue of seniority— a system which again works to the disadvantage of urban constituencies. Much positive legislation receiving both presidential and major party support can easily be blocked by individuals or committees that are least reflective of and responsive to national public opinion. The major consequences of this imbalance of power have been well summarized by a close student of Congress, Professor James Burns, in these words:

The total effect of unfair districting, unrepresentative committees, the seniority rule, and obstructionism in Congress is fourfold:

(1) They prevent Congress from reflecting more fairly the sentiment of the people as a whole. In general the rural population and producer interests are over-represented, urban groups and consumer interests are under-represented.

(2) They often stop Congress from acting at all. The filibuster, although it can be used to gain support for some measure, is essentially a negative instrument, a means of blocking action. So is the power of the committee chairman: he can frustrate action by his fellow committee members, but he cannot so easily expedite a measure.

(3) They weaken Congress further as an instrument of majority rule. Blocs representing localities, sections, and special interests take advantage of the organization and rules of each house to hamstring the disorganized, undisciplined majority.

(4) They intensify the problem of the separation of powers between executive and legislative branches. As a result of these factors Congress speaks for a different constellation of forces than does the President. Congress often evades the supreme job of democratic government, which is the adjustment of differences among groups in order to find the basis for joint action by at least a majority. Nor does it feel impelled to go along with the programs of President or party.[6]

An interesting case example of the above conclusions can be found in Professor Burns's account of price control legislation passed early in World War II. The original proposals, backed by both the President and administration leaders in Congress, met stiff opposition from the farm bloc, which controlled the crucial committee posts. The bill that finally passed both houses was so buttressed with provisos designed to protect agriculture that Senator Alben Barkley, the majority leader, sardonically termed it a "farm relief measure."[7]

Though the forces shaping legislation are usually difficult to delineate with precision, it seems clear that disproportionate rural influence is a major factor behind much congressional action and inaction. Since the most important sources of this power inhere in the committee and seniority systems, these deserve to be discussed in more detail.

The internal organization of both houses of Congress is characterized by a thorough decentralization of power among numerous standing committees. The major decisions of legislative policy are made in the various committees, which generally hold the power of life or death for proposed statutes. Hence the very make-up of a commitee is of crucial importance.

Within each committee the decisive role is played by the chairman, who in most cases can direct the legislative traffic as he sees fit. These powerful positions are allocated on the basis of seniority, with each party's committee membership ranked according to continuous service. For both parties the rise to power and influence is determined mainly by the ability to be re-elected. This system automatically places senators and representatives from "safe" states or districts at an enormous advantage. While there are some exceptions, the "safe" constituencies for each party are usually rural. Fluid and changing urban districts are more likely to be closely contested two-party areas which reflect more accurately newer and changing political tides. The system favors those congressmen who are least compelled to face strong competition on the basis of fresh issues. It renders a corresponding advantage to those economic interests that find support in the politically "safe" constituencies, where there is little chance of a turnover of representatives. Committee chairmen are invariably politicians whose own districts have remained insulated from any periodic transformations in the national political climate.

A glance at the committee rosters of any session of Congress will quickly reveal the preponderance of rural power. Ranking Democrats are usually from Southern rural areas, while the senior Republicans tend to represent rural constituencies of the Middle West, and the Northeast. This pattern holds true for both houses, but especially for the House of Representatives, due to its more parochial basis. Seldom does a committee chairmanship go to a representative from a thriving metropolitan area. The roster of the eighty-third Congress shows that of the thirty-eight House committee chairmen and ranking minority members only two (both Democrats) represented large metropolitan districts (New York and Chicago). Absent from so lofty a position on the committee hierarchy were representatives from such larger cities as Philadelphia, Los Angeles, Detroit, Baltimore, Cleveland, St. Louis, Boston, San Francisco, Pittsburgh, and Milwaukee—to mention only some of the more populous.

In addition to holding a controlling share of committee chairmanships, rural forces often fare exceptionally well in the total representation on the more important committees. For example, the crucial Rules Committee of the House of Representatives usually reflects a definite rural preponderance.

The committee structure of Congress places a large portion of the nation's decision-making in the hands of individuals and groups least responsive to the needs of a modern industrialized society. An increasing amount of national legislation encompasses problems of primary concern to urban inhabitants—housing, civil defense, labor, and business policies, to mention a few. Yet the internal organization of Congress leaves that body poorly equipped to handle these vital problems with adequate understanding. Furthermore, the local and unduly rural bias of Congress helps explain the wide gulf that so often separates the legislature from an executive branch inevitably more concerned with nation-wide issues.

State Legislatures and Amending the Constitution

It is a well-established proposition that the process for amending the United States Constitution is extremely difficult. One intention of the framers, fearful of the "excesses of democracy," was to institute a check on the popular majority so that a change would require almost overwhelming support. As a result, constitutional growth since the eighteenth century has been largely accomplished by less formal means such as judicial review, the party system, and presidential powers.

The Constitution requires that amendments be proposed by a two-thirds vote of both houses of Congress or by a national convention called by Congress on the application of legislatures in three-fourths of the states; proposed amendments must be ratified by three-fourths of the state legislatures or special conventions, whichever Congress decides upon. Due to the complexities of the procedure, only twenty-two amendments have been passed since 1789, and the first ten can be considered as virtually part of the original Constitution.

The amending process is still important, however, and the participation of the states is worthy of attention. Since state legislatures are in a position to petition Congress for amendments and are usually called upon to decide their ratification, the make-up of these bodies is once again important. While a preponderant popular sentiment may be desirable for basic changes in the governmental framework, the obvious question is: How well do state legislatures serve as barometers of public opinion? Some indication has already been provided in Chapter Three.

The question of representation in state legislatures has frequently played an important role in the history of the national amending process. After the Civil War, unsuccessful attempts were made to secure submission of the Thirteenth and Fifteenth amendments to state conventions instead of to the legislatures, due to doubts concerning the representative nature of state law-making bodies. The rural-urban issue came to the fore during the campaign for prohibition of liquor, which resulted in the adoption of the Eighteenth Amendment in 1919. Most "dry" sentiment was located in rural areas, while cities were generally "wet." Spokesmen for the Anti-Saloon League publicly asserted that the proposed amendment must pass Congress before 1920, when a prospective reapportionment of the lower house in accordance with population changes would result in some forty new "wet" representatives.

The only break with the tradition of allowing state legislatures to assume responsibility for ratification came with the repeal of the prohibition amendment. The "wets" had apparently not forgotten the importance of rural-dominated legislative bodies. Consequently the convention method was chosen by Congress as one which would allow a more representative opinion in the states.

Many believed that the adoption of the Twenty-first Amendment through the convention technique had brought into vogue a more democratic ratification method. However, the eightieth Congress reverted to the process of state legislative ratification for the Twenty-second Amendment, limiting presidential tenure to two terms (adopted in 1951). The reason should not be difficult to detect in view of the partisan implications of the third-term issue in recent years. State legislatures could be expected to view the matter in a somewhat different light than would popular conventions. While the Amendment passed thirty-six state legislatures (with little debate or discussion), it is safe to say that there was scant public awareness of this basic Constitutional change until ratification had been accomplished.

The very nature of the amending process has acted as a barrier to attempted changes of a liberal nature. The large majorities needed both within Congress and among the states have allowed rural minorities to wield decisive vetoes. Recent trends, however, indicate that the difficulties are far fewer for conservative groups.

An interesting case in point is the recent attempt to limit severely the scope and extent of the Sixteenth (income tax) Amendment. The campaign apparently began in 1938 with the American Taxpayers Association, Inc., an offspring of the Committee for Constitutional Government. The purpose was to limit federal income tax to a maximum of 25 per cent on any amount of income. The effect would obviously be a marked shift in the tax burden from high-income groups to low-income groups. Congress, faced with the responsibility of obtaining adequate revenue for a large-scale budget, has shown little enthusiasm for an arbitrary ceiling on income taxation. Interests sponsoring the restriction found more responsive audiences in state legislatures.

By 1952 some twenty-eight state legislatures had recommended to Congress the calling of a convention to limit the income tax, though seven of these later rescinded their actions. Similar proposals also passed a single house in at least nine additional states. If a total of thirty-two state legislatures pass the application, Congress may call a convention. It is clear that the nature and consequences of the proposed tax limit were not publicized or debated in the states whose legislatures passed the proposal. Since the result would be higher taxes for most taxpayers, it seems reasonable to assume that the measure, if understood, would not receive the overwhelming support supposedly needed for a constitutional amendment.

Regardless of the disposition of the campaign for income tax revision, the potential power held by state legislatures is sufficiently clear. While it was once assumed that federal amendments required a preponderant and highly active public support, it may now be necessary to revise this generalization. It now appears that certain moves for amendment may pass through state legislatures almost without notice. Nor is this reversal so unusual as it may appear. Formerly most serious campaigns for constitutional amendments were progressive in nature, designed to remove or modify some of the restrictions on majority rule. More recently, especially since the federal government has assumed a more active role in the national economy, minority property interests appear to seek protection in the amending clause. In such a situation, unrepresentative state legislatures provide an access to those groups that find less success at the national level.

In view of the impact of state legislatures on national institutions as well as on state and local policies, the time has clearly arrived for a much-needed reassessment of their adequacies. State lawmaking bodies claim moral authority to pass laws for public observance, and act otherwise on behalf of the states' citizens. Their role then is—or should be—a representative one.

CHAPTER SIX

A Critique

The preceding chapters have described the patterns of urban and rural representation and their consequences at various levels of government. Useful as it is to examine closely the particular state, municipal, and federal ramifications, such partial compartmentalization should not obscure the general characteristics of a problem that cuts across formal institutional arrangements. As the discussion thus far has already indicated, a realistic analysis of rural and urban political power must recognize the interrelationships and interdependence of the so-called "levels" of government. The nature of contemporary American federalism points up the inadequacy of treating its problems in isolation. Patterns of political power do not confine themselves to one or another governmental unit, but rather weave through the whole federal fabric.

A broad view of American politics today reveals a general situation of inflated rural power. It is one of the basic contributing causes for much of the stalemate that has become so characteristic of our political life. Of tremendous significance is the fact that the rural-urban split finds a close parallel in the constitutional separation of powers. The legislative branch, both state and (to a lesser degree) national, reflects the strong influence of rural and small-town constituencies. Yet the executive is more often representative of the new urban majorities. This explains much of the fundamental antagonism so often evident between President and Congress, between governor and state legislature. The result is a check and balance system with a vengeance. A question of obvious importance is whether the ever-accelerating problems of an urban, industrial society can be adequately met by political machinery whose design seems more suited to an earlier, simpler, and far different era.

As we have seen earlier, the representative basis and internal organization of Congress bring about a rural-based legislative leadership. The allocation of such positions of power as committee chairmanships greatly favors lawmakers from constituencies least affected by the ebb and flow of vigorous political currents. The dramatic rise over the past generation of an urban America has had a far less direct effect on Congress than on the executive.

As a result, policies embodied in national legislation often bear the stamp of this imbalance. As the United States has entered—belatedly but actively —the stage of world affairs, the adequacy of our policy-making machinery has become an ever more crucial question. The impact of domestic political behavior on foreign relations as well as internal problems must not be overlooked or underestimated.

In view of the varying degrees of influence exerted by national leaders, we need to know far more than we do about the social and political backgrounds of our decision-makers. It seems a plausible hypothesis that many important legislative leaders trace their rise to influence through a system that—from bottom to top—gives an advantage to rural, small-town districts. The patterns of power already established in the various states permeate our national politics, both formally and informally. The decentralization of the American party system lends itself to the perpetuation of many locally oriented characteristics, for the power structure of a state political party often mirrors the formal legislative pattern.

While much of our federal and state governmental apparatus seems intent on ignoring or minimizing the special problems of an industrial civilization, municipal units must constantly cope with them. They do so usually under considerable handicaps. Their appeals for greater autonomy or state assistance have often fallen upon deaf ears. The growing interrelationships of cities and federal agencies is partially a consequence of slow and inadequate state policies. For the federal government, in spite of the situation in Congress, is still considerably more representative of urban interests than are most state legislatures. Those officials of state governments who decry the trend toward "centralization" have not far to look for some of its causes.

Federalism and "States' Rights"

Recent years have seen an increasing interest and concern in some quarters over the proper scope and authority of state vis-à-vis federal government. In 1953 President Eisenhower appointed a Commission on Inter-Governmental Relations to study this general problem, as well as all aspects of federal aid programs. Many state spokesmen have called for transfer of certain federal activities and taxing powers to the states. It is not surprising that some city officials view such proposals with suspicion and misgivings. They fear that proponents of decentralization wish to stop at the state level rather than continue the shift of power to localities. The terms "states' rights" and "local self-government" are far from synonymous. Certainly the representative nature of state governments is a vital question, prerequisite to any serious consideration of a shifting of powers. No study commission can hope to resolve the issues of federalism and decentralization without first facing up to the widespread extent of urban under-representation in state legislatures.

The issue of "states' rights" must also be viewed in a context of group interests and their varying degrees of influence on government. In the light of political patterns prevalent at the state level, it is not surprising that certain economic interests wish decisions to be made there rather than by agencies of the federal government. State legislatures offer avenues of access and influence to groups that are far less powerful at other levels. Proposals to shift control of certain phases of economic life from federal agencies to state governments often mean in reality an abandonment or relaxation of controls. An example is indicated in the recent controversy over a proposed transfer of federal coal mine safety inspection to the states.

The controversy over urban and rural political representation can be fully understood only when it is viewed in terms of political power. Once the nature of the problem is recognized, much of the discussion and debate that so often surround the issue can be seen as misleading, irrelevant, or based on superficial insights into the political process.

The defenders of unequal representation generally base their arguments on a number of implicit assumptions that bear re-examination. One of these regards localities, such as counties, as distinct communities of interest. It is asserted that legislative representation must recognize all of the various regions and communities in such a way that a few urban centers cannot dominate state political affairs. The so-called "balance" and "federal" plans, by which minority population areas are given control of one house while the other more directly represents numbers, are usually defended as protecting all segments of the state's population against the majority. Yet it is a one-way argument. The proposition is never heard that heavily rural states should allow a small minority of cities to control one house of the legislature. This would be no more justified by democratic theory than the reverse, but it would follow from the logic of the "balance" concept. Giving area special consideration in one house while the other house represents population appears superficially to be a fair arrangement. Yet the central issue, beclouded by the nature of bicameralism, is obscured. The result of "balance" plans is that groups with less popular support gain an inordinate bargaining power, while measures having wide public support are as easily defeated in one house as two. Certainly it is clear that such "compromise" schemes have not resolved or avoided intense antagonisms in the states where they have operated. Ohio, California, and New Jersey are a few examples.

The argument in favor of giving special recognition to various regions of a state through area representation often rests on the assumption that political boundaries conform to social or community boundaries. While this was largely true in the eighteenth century (and possibly later in some parts of the nation), it is hardly a tenable premise today. The early concept of representation assumed that representatives could actually speak for the small and highly homogeneous communities which then existed. A community was both a geographical and a socio-economic unit, with a high degree of autonomy and relatively little contact with other localities. Thus individual and regional interests could be considered as largely identical. This simple form of community has long since been displaced. The rapid and dynamic changes wrought by industrialization have ushered in new ecological patterns that scarcely parallel old political boundaries.

Surely it cannot be seriously suggested today that county or legislative districts actually correspond to distinct social communities. In nearly all cases political boundaries are necessarily arbitrary, drawn for the sake of convenience. Economic and social interests usually transcend county and even state lines. One glance at a map of the New York City metropolitan area reveals in dramatic fashion how artificial are state, county, and township boundaries in an area where natural ecological development has spread over parts of three states and numerous subunits of government. Similar situations exist, though not so intensively, in all sections of the United States. While the disparity is especially noticeable for urban areas, even rural regions show little distinct correlation between political and social units. The doctrine of community interests is reminiscent of the theory set forth in the nineteenth century by John C. Calhoun, who insisted that government must represent a majority of interests (assumed to be bounded by state lines) instead of numbers. What was brilliantly abstract but out of touch with reality even in Calhoun's day is far less tenable in the complex urban society of the twentieth century.

Majority Rule and Minority Rights

A closely related issue thus arises regarding the question of majority rule and minority rights. Defenders of rural overrepresentation assert that less populated areas deserve proportionately greater influence as a means of protecting themselves against a tyrannical urban majority. It is quite true that democratic theory is concerned with minority rights as well as majority rule. Yet does the protection of minorities necessitate yielding either control or a veto power to them? If so, then the traditional principles of majority rule must be abandoned.

Furthermore, the case for rural minority rights rests on an assumption that cities constitute, singly or in combination, a cohesive political force. Yet does this square with reality? Do all, or even most, urban centers in a state function as unanimous forces in the body politic? Experience indicates a negative answer. After all, cities are divided on political matters; none constitutes a single and distinct group in regard to social and economic policies. The fears expressed over possible city domination of legislative bodies betray an inadequate understanding of the nature of modern society.

Nor are defenders of rural power alone in oversimplifying the problem. Indeed, the traditional case in favor of equal representation also envisages the issue in terms of a majority-minority dichotomy that by itself is now inadequate and misleading. When Jefferson protested in the eighteenth century against a system of representation in which "every man in Warwick has as much influence in the government as seventeen in Loudon" he spoke the language of classical individualism. In that day such an approach seemed to make good sense. It was assumed that there was a direct connection between each "political man" and his representative and that his weight in the political process could be measured in terms of individual interests. The ideal of political equality was naturally translated into the corollary principle of equal representation. This orientation has likewise characterized, to a large extent, the traditional analyses by political scientists and others interested in the problem of representation. The assertion that one person in county A has four, six, or thirty times the weight as each person in county B is still a telling point.

The complexity of the political process, especially in the twentieth century, calls for a re-examination of some of the premises underlying former theories. A realistic approach to the problem of representation today must go beyond the terminology of individualism and consider the relevance of group dynamics in the political process. The principle of equal representation still merits a solid justification, but for reasons that must be stated in different terms from those of eighteenth- and nineteenth-century political theorists.

If we regard society in terms of group interests we can approach the question of majorities and minorities more meaningfully. The so-called urban majority is simply an aggregate of people representing any number of distinct (and often politically antagonistic) groups. It was observed earlier that some urban business interests make political alliances with certain rural forces rather than with other urban interests. This is just one indication of important group cleavages. While rural society is usually more homogeneous, it too has important internal differences. For instance, in many states there is a variance in broad political outlook between farmers and the rural smalltown elements, though courthouse "rings" of the latter usually monopolize political leadership for the whole area.

While public policy is consequently the result of multigroup pulls and pressures, the concrete legislative issues involved must be decided in terms of majorities and minorities within the lawmaking body itself. In this sense it is true that on certain questions more urban representatives may take a different position from that of most rural legislators. However, this stage is only the final one in a complex process and tends to obscure earlier negotiations reached as a result of the political power pattern. Furthermore, as regards actual cohesiveness, legislators from the countryside have a wide-spread reputation for a far higher degree of solidarity than those representing cities, where articulate group interests are more diversified. In some states a high degree of urban solidarity might be expected on particular municipal problems as distinguished from broad, statewide social and economic issues. For instance, there could conceivably be an "urban bloc" on such matters as grants-in-aid to cities, home rule, local tax powers and the like (though many mayors complain that even here unity among urban legislators is lacking). In such a situation it seems logical that urban areas should have a proportionate voice. It is true that an urban majority in this sense might abuse its powers just as any majority might. But the answer hardly seems to be minority rule and abuse. If discrimination is ever likely on some issues, then at least it seems the lesser of evils to confine its scope to as few persons as possible.

The Fear of Urban Tyranny

The complexity of the situation renders the chance of "urban tyranny" highly improbable if equal representation did exist. In those few states, such as Massachusetts, where equitable urban-rural representation has prevailed in modern times there has been no evidence that legislators representing urban majorities have acted in concert to exploit the rest of the state. In most states there is a degree of rivalry among cities in addition to the differences within each of them. For example, San Francisco and Los Angeles can hardly be expected to send solidly allied delegations to the California legislature; and within each city are party, factional, social, economic, and other differences that hardly comprise one big urban interest. In the few instances where one urban area contains a majority of the state population, there is likewise no reasonable ground for believing that this center would—or, indeed, could—act as a single organic entity in "controlling" the legislature. Such a fear neglects the complexity of political and social structure that is particularly evident in metropolitan areas. The professed apprehensions of downstate Illinois at possible Cook County "domination" are groundless in view of the marked difference in social and political outlook between Chicago city and the suburban area of the county, to mention one obvious cleavage. In New York state, party allegiance has been a more persuasive determinant of legislators' behavior than their loyalty to local interests. The 1954 revenue fight found city Republicans allied with fellow Republicans upstate in opposition to the city's "official" attitude.

While a granting of urban representation proportionate to population would not result in a single, cohesive urban "majority," it could effectuate a considerable shift in the pattern of political power. Some urban interests that formerly had little influence would probably gain more, while others (notably those that enjoy an advantage from an alliance with rural forces) would lose. It is this potential shift in the power equilibrium that arouses the greatest resistance from the elements benefiting from the status quo. That resistance is prompted by a fear not of *an* urban interest, but of *certain* urban interests.

An imbalance of representative strength, then, means that accessibility to the decision-making process is rendered difficult or impossible for some groups and easier for others. Interests that have greater influence in constituencies with inflated power possess an obvious advantage over those whose support comes from areas that are underrepresented. Jefferson's classic example ("every man in Warwick has as much influence as seventeen in Loudon") translates into contemporary terms something like this: those interests with influence in Warwick have an advantage over those interests whose support is confined to Loudon. But in spite of a change in terminology, equal representation is as essential to modern democracy as it was in an earlier day. Only under such a system can governmental structure be considered as allowing all significant groups a maximum degree of accessibility to the decision-making process.

An Ethical Question

The problem of representation, however, involves more than just the institutions of government, whether state, local, or national. There is a less tangible and less publicized element involving psychological attitudes of the public. It seems clear that a continual disregard of professed ideals (and often of constitutional principles as well) engenders a sense of frustration and injustice. Double standards of political morality throughout much of the nation contribute to a climate of public cynicism and apathy.

In recent years the whole question of ethics in relation to government has come forcibly to public view. Attention has usually centered upon the more dramatic examples, such as overt or subtle bribery, the seeking and dispensing of favors, quick profits from government loans, and similar incidents. Often overlooked is the more general problem which involves conflicting and contradictory codes of conduct in all parts of society. While it has seldom been considered in such a light, the variance between democratic theory and undemocratic practices involved in state legislative representation indicates a deeper ethical problem. Its solution constitutes an important challenge to contemporary American institutions and values.

CHAPTER SEVEN

Is There a Solution?

It is easier to demonstrate the nature and consequences of unbalanced representation than it is to suggest workable solutions to the problem. While the question involves the very basis of government and becomes increasingly important, the obstacles to change are formidable. In most states there seems little hope for more democratically based legislatures. In fact, the trend over recent years (with a few encouraging exceptions) has been in the direction of even greater degrees of urban underrepresentation. In what directions might one look for partial solutions?

Judicial Remedies

In view of America's tradition of a written constitution and a powerful judiciary, it is not surprising that attempted solutions have frequently taken the form of legal appeals. As has been mentioned earlier, numerous cases invoking an enforcement of state constitutions have been of no avail. State courts have consistently refused to intervene with the legislature's failure to reapportion. Failing judicial remedies on the state level, interested urban groups have considered turning to the federal courts on the basis of various sections of the United States Constitution. In 1931 a unique test case arose when a citizen of Illinois refused to pay his federal income tax on the ground that the United States government had failed to guarantee a republican form of government and thus had ceased to have authority in Illinois. A federal district court was not impressed by this reasoning and followed the traditional judicial reluctance to attempt a definition of "republican form of government."

In recent years the United States Conference of Mayors has threatened to bring a carefully selected case to the federal courts on the ground that inferior urban representation is a denial by the state of equal protection of the laws guaranteed by the Fourteenth Amendment. Prospects for success here seem dim at least in the foreseeable future. The closest occasion for including representative equality under the Fourteenth Amendment came in the leading case of *Colegrove v. Green* in 1945. There a liberal interpretation of the equal protection clause was persuasive for a minority of three justices as opposed to a four-man majority which was split on the reasoning employed. This case concerned the gross disparities in the size of congressional districts in Illinois. Declaring that such a condition was not a matter for judicial determination, the court concluded with the futile suggestion that "the remedy for unfairness in districting is to secure State Legislatures that will apportion properly, or to invoke the ample power of Congress."[1] In the minority opinion Mr. Justice Black felt that the equal protection clause of the Fourteenth Amendment forbade such discrimination. A state, he insisted, would not be permitted to pick out one group of citizens and deny them the vote altogether, or to allot expressly a half-vote to some citizens and a full vote to others. Yet, grossly unequal apportionments have the same effect. "Such discriminatory legislation seems to me exactly the kind that the equal protection clause was intended to prohibit."[2] It was a mere "play upon words," Black continued, to term such a controversy as "political" in the sense that "courts have nothing to do with protecting and vindicating the right of a voter to cast an effective ballot." Probably alarmed at the closeness of the decision, the Illinois legislature has since established a more equitable congressional apportionment. While it is possible that the dissent in the Colegrove case may eventually become law, such a shift in the Court's interpretation seems unlikely for some time. Since the Supreme Court is this reluctant to interfere with congressional districting it would doubtless be even more reluctant to invalidate an unrepresentative apportionment for the state legislature, in spite of Justice Black's reminder that the latter situation was responsible for the former and that both were thus interdependent.

Institutional Improvements

There are a number of possible actions that are worthy of consideration under this category. One that has received increasing attention recently is the extension of "compulsory" or "automatic" reapportionment plans. This generally means that responsibility for periodic changes in representation is shifted from the legislature to an executive or judicial body which could approach the matter with a greater degree of objectivity. The method of enforcement varies among the states that have adopted "compulsory" schemes. In some cases, such as in California, South Dakota, and Texas, the provision for an executive commission to redistrict in the event of legislative inaction, has served as a spur to the lawmakers. The legislature's jealousy of allowing another branch to assume the redistricting function apparently insures quick action. An established formula requiring only mathematical computations by officials from the executive branch is used for redistricting the lower houses of Ohio and Missouri. This same board in Ohio (governor, auditor, and secretary of state) also redistricts the senate, though some discretion here is necessarily allowed. In Missouri the governor appoints the senate redistricting board composed of an equal number from each of the major political parties. The purpose is obviously that of eliminating or minimizing potential gerrymanders. Arkansas is of special interest because of the judiciary's role. While apportionment is entrusted to the executive branch, the state supreme court is held in reserve, in the event of inaction or abuse of discretion. The court can then issue mandamus proceedings or revise the apportionment scheme on its own motion. The judicial apportionment of 1952 in Arkansas appears equitable and much superior to usual legislative jobs.

A number of models for automatic reapportionment are now available. States in which reapportionment is a chronic headache should consider the merits of an automatic decennial plan which either removes the function entirely from the legislature or operates in the event of that body's inaction. The fact that several states have adopted some form of compulsory reapportionment would seem to indicate less resistance from legislatures than might ordinarily be expected. A number of legislators who find it difficult to cooperate personally in redistricting when party, constituency, or friends are due to suffer, are willing to entrust the task to an outside agency.

However, representative legislatures are not possible in most states even with automatic or compulsory reapportionment plans, since constitutional provisions usually limit the representation of more populous areas in at least one house. In these states urban centers must be content with an arrangement that at least keeps the legislature from becoming more unrepresentative.

Another institutional improvement would be a realistic and comprehensive consolidation of counties in many states. At the same time this is one of the most difficult accomplishments to envisage. In several states the county has attained an almost sovereign status through its overrepresentation in the legislature. Small, rural counties with a disproportionately large share of seats will not gracefully yield their prerogatives. Not only does this situation impede plans to modernize the archaic structure of county government, but it also helps perpetuate the rotten borough characteristics of so many state legislatures. In view of these conditions, it is disquieting to observe the frequent attempts to grant individual counties an even larger share of legislative power than they already have. So-called "federal" plans, allowing each county an equal or nearly equal status in one house, are proposed with increasing regularity, sometimes with success. The weakness of the attempted analogy to the United States Senate has been discussed earlier. Yet the phrase "federal" is effectively exploited by opponents of democratic representation.

If area considerations must be used as a legislative basis, there is one possible method that would still provide equitable representation. This would be to pattern the state legislature upon federal congressional districts, with an equal number of state legislators chosen from each district. (This scheme would not be applicable to less populous states with few congressional districts.) It would be possible to employ a system of proportional representation as advocated by the National Municipal League in its model state constitution, or some variant such as the minority representation scheme used for the lower house in Illinois. The use of congressional districts would have the virtue of simplicity and equitability. At the same time it might satisfy at least partially the traditional emphasis on a geographic area. Since congressional candidates would be chosen from the same districts some sense of political community might be developed, as well as a partial integration of local and national politics. A prerequisite for the success of this plan would be an assurance that congressional districts are reasonably equal and easily redrawn to reflect population shifts.

The Initiative

In a minority of states there is one possible method of by-passing recalcitrant legislatures: the initiative. Thirteen states[3] include the initiative as part of the constitutional amending process as well as for direct legislation; six additional states[4] restrict the initiative to legislation only. The availability of this instrument of popular control in some of these states is modified, but in most the problem of representation could probably be dealt with.

In 1952, Oregon became the fourth state in which the initiative was successfully directed toward the problem of representation. In two of these states the initiative campaign passed direct reapportionment statutes only, while in the other two constitutional amendments were carried. The ground was broken in Washington state by a successful initiative campaign in 1930, which stands as the state's only reapportionment in half a century. The Colorado electorate followed suit in 1932 after a legislative failure of two decades. In 1936 a constitutional initiative in Arkansas transferred the apportionment duty from the legislature (which had not acted since 1890) to a board of reapportionment and to the state supreme court as a final resort. In the more recent case of Oregon, a carefully drafted constitutional amendment enforces decennial reapportionment by placing that duty with the secretary of state in the event of legislative failure, with an added guarantee of judicial review. It also stipulated details for a temporary reapportionment (the state's first in some forty years) to serve until the regular method takes effect after the 1960 federal census.

These successful cases must be contrasted with the ill-fated initiative

campaign of 1948 in California. Here an attempt to modify the grossly
unrepresentative senate was soundly defeated even in the urban areas that
would have gained representation by the change. The failure in California
can be attributed in large part to a lack of broad-based support and the
formidable opposition of influential interests, including most newspapers.
In the four states where the initiative was successfully employed, conditions
were far more favorable for passage.

While the initiative is often a cumbersome and expensive process, it
serves as an alternative medium for groups that find themselves at a disadvantage in the legislature. There is a current tendency among many political scientists to be somewhat critical of direct legislation as being
damaging to the strength and responsibility of the legislature. Yet such
objections assume that the legislature is a representative body, which is
usually not the case. The constitutional initiative, if wisely constructed, has
a special merit of circumventing a legislative monopoly on structural and
other changes. As urban underrepresentation continues to become more
accentuated, a particularly good case can be made for the initiative. As
imperfect as it is for "recording the popular will" it at least allows possible
alternative channels of representation for groups denied a proper voice in
the regular law-making bodies. At any rate, in those states where the
initiative process is available there is an important possible solution to
legislative inaction on the problem of representation.

The Problem of Change

The readjustment of representative institutions to meet the realities of
twentieth-century society is an obvious need. Yet there is little cause for
optimism. Perhaps the most basic obstacle is the inflexibility of our institutions to allow for change. The crux of the problem is the state legislature
itself. In many instances its practices of malapportionment have been
responsible for a situation of unequal representation. There is usually no
popular control so long as the lawmaking body reflects a distorted image
of the public. Where the main reason for representative inequality is the
state constitution, the possible avenues of change are again usually blocked
by the position of the legislature. It is this body that is usually vested with
the responsibility for initiating constitutional revision. Legislative self-
interest militates against any change in its own status or make-up.

This situation gives rise to the basic question of whether the legislature
is a sovereign body or a representative one. It is generally assumed in
American states that the people are sovereign and that governmental units
act in a representative capacity. Yet the gap between theory and practice
is a wide one. In about two-thirds of the states all amendments to the
constitution must originate with the legislature. Exceptions are the thirteen

where the initiative is available, plus a few more where the electorate periodically has an opportunity to vote for a constitutional convention. Most conventions, however, are patterned largely upon legislative representation, so that any existing inequalities are usually projected into the body charged with revising the constitution. Any possibility of a truly representative convention invariably results in refusal by the legislature to authorize the calling of such a group. Georgia's constitution of 1945 was drawn up by an appointed commission whose work was subject to legislative revision before being submitted to popular vote. No constitutional change by the convention method seemed possible due to legislative fear of a popularly-based group which might tamper with representation or the county-unit system. New Jersey secured a new constitution in 1947 after years of agitation only when the legislature authorized a "limited" convention which was prohibited at the outset from even discussing the question of legislative representation.

The practical barriers to changes in governmental institutions contrast markedly with the theories underlying state constitutions themselves. Invariably these charters contain some statement to the effect that "all political power is vested in and derived from the people." A good many add provisos to the effect that the "people" or a majority reserve the right to alter or abolish the government whenever they deem it necessary to their safety and happiness. The New Hampshire constitution adds with unusual vehemence: "The doctrine of nonresistance against arbitrary power and oppression, is absurd, slavish, and destructive of the good and happiness of mankind."

The American concept that sovereignty is popular and that all governmental institutions are accountable to that sovereign has inspired some suggestions for extralegal procedures when legal requirements themselves contradict the basic theory. No urban groups have gone so far as to assert the right of revolution against unrepresentative state governments, though Chicago officials once came close to that point. But a former president of the United States Conference of Mayors suggested as recently as 1949 that "a few Boston Tea Parties in some of our states might serve a useful purpose."[5] In this same line of reasoning, some have suggested the possibility of bypassing recalcitrant and unrepresentative legislatures for such matters as calling constitutional conventions. This approach assumes broad and active public support as well as leadership by some representatives (such as the governor) of the public at large. This type of action was urged during the years when New Jersey's rotten-borough senate consistently stymied every attempt to secure a much-needed revision of the constitution. One suggestion—that the representative lower house might alone assert the right to call a constitutional convention—was attributed to Arthur Vanderbilt, former president of the American Bar Association and later chief justice of New Jersey.

Such situations attest to a lamentable break-down in the adequacy of legal procedures in providing for needed change. That crises do not occur more frequently is probably due to public apathy and lack of interest in the problem in many states. A reassessment of representative practices and their relationship to democratic ideals is imperative. Frustration, friction, disinterest, and cynicism result from the fact that institutional forms in so many cases violate the professed values and norms of our society. Democracy, majority rule, and political equality are all held up as ideals, but they are far from realized in practice.

As American society becomes increasingly urban and industrialized, it can ill afford to depend upon attitudes and institutions that are unadaptable. A greater awareness of the nature and consequences of rural and urban patterns of political power is clearly needed. While it is difficult—and unwise—to retain the optimism of eighteenth-century democrats toward the possibility of complete rationality in human conduct, it would be even less wise to admit an incapacity for the self-direction that is urgently needed. Superficial explanations and inherited prejudices must eventually give way to a realistic and comprehensive understanding of political behavior if our urban society is to evolve an effective solution to the problem of representation.

Footnotes to the Study

Chapter One

1. A. Whitney Griswold: *Democracy and Farming*, New Haven, Yale University Press, 1952, p. 137.

2. Lane Lancaster: *Government in Rural America*, 2d ed., New York, D. Van Nostrand Company, Inc., 1952, pp. 57–58.

3. Jefferson to William King, 19 November 1819, Jefferson Papers, Library of Congress, Vol. 216, p. 38616.

Chapter Two

1. Judge Simeon S. Willis in *Stiglitz v. Schardien*, 239 Ky. at 812 (1931).

2. *The Writings of Thomas Jefferson*, Library Edition, Washington, D.C., 1903, Vol. II, pp. 160–61.

3. Quoted in Robert Luce: *Legislative Principles*, Boston, Houghton Mifflin Company, 1930, p. 344.

4. Max Farrand (ed.): *The Records of the Federal Convention of 1787*, New Haven, Yale University Press, 1911, Vol. I, p. 185.

5. *Ibid.*, p. 562.

6. Quoted in Luce, *op. cit.*, pp. 346–47.

Chapter Three

1. Factual data on legislative representation for the various states are based upon the most recent materials, including constitutions, manuals, etc., provided by the secretary of state or other responsible official in each of the forty-eight states. Computations involving population figures are based on the 1950 federal census.

Chapter Four

1. Conclusions and information in the first part of this chapter are based partially upon a more extensive survey reported in Gordon E. Baker: "Cities Resent Stepchild Lot," *National Municipal Review*, 42:387–92 (September 1953). Statements by mayors Zeidler and Henderson are taken from letters to the author. Brochures published by the United States Conference of Mayors provided some factual data as well as attitudes. Helpful on municipal financial struggles was the lead article of the *Wall Street Journal*, November 10, 1953, p. 1.

2. New York *Times*, October 23, 1953, p. 18.

3. New York *Times*, February 4, 1954, p. 1.

Chapter Five

1. Congressional district population figures are taken from the *Congressional Directory* for the 83d Congress, 2d session.

2. Quoted in Joel Paschal: "The House of Representatives: 'Grand Depository of the Democratic Principle'?" *Law and Contemporary Problems*, 17:276–89 (Spring 1952).

3. Quoted in *Ibid.*, p. 278.

4. Quoted in *Congressional Quarterly*, 10:463 (May 1952).

5. Quoted in New York *Times*, December 6, 1951, p. 26.

6. James MacGregor Burns: *Congress on Trial*, New York, Harper & Brothers, 1949, p. 65.

7. Quoted in *Ibid.*, p. 89.

Chapter Seven

1. *Colegrove v. Green*, 328 U.S. at 556.

2. *Ibid.*, at 569.

3. Arizona, Arkansas, California, Colorado, Massachusetts, Michigan, Missouri, Nebraska, Nevada, North Dakota, Ohio, Oklahoma, and Oregon.

4. Idaho, Montana, South Dakota, Utah, Washington, and Maine (very modified).

5. Speech by George Welch, former mayor of Grand Rapids, Michigan, quoted in Robert S. Allen (ed.): *Our Sovereign State*, New York, Vanguard Press, Inc., 1949, p. xxii.

Bibliographical Note

While the importance of urban-rural conflict is acknowledged in many studies of American politics, there has been surprisingly little published in the way of detailed analysis on the subject. Only a few articles have appeared on the general nature and extent of the problem, and these are now largely outdated. Useful references to the pattern of rural power in one section of the nation appear in V. O. Key's *Southern Politics* (New York, Alfred A. Knopf, Inc., 1949). Wesley McCune's *The Farm Bloc* (Garden City, N.Y., Doubleday, Doran and Co., 1943), while giving only incidental mention to the representative imbalance, shows the power exerted nationally by rural-based groups, as well as the close support they receive from certain urban business interests. Samuel Lubell's *The Future of American Politics* (New York, Harper & Brothers, 1951) is full of insights concerning the general impact of urbanization upon national political behavior, though there is little direct mention of representation. Alfred de Grazia, *Public and Republic* (New York, Alfred A. Knopf, Inc., 1951) is concerned with the theory of representation, but deals only incidentally with the urban-rural problem. A gold mine of early historical data on representation and apportionment will be found in Robert Luce's *Legislative Principles* (Cambridge, Houghton Mifflin Company, 1930), especially chapters 15 and 16. The most complete treatment of apportionment is the Spring 1952 issue of *Law and Contemporary Problems*, entitled "Legislative Reapportionment." This work contains articles of varying quality and utility, but must be used with caution due to the large amount of factual misinformation contained in some of the contributions. The report of the American Political Science Association's Committee on American Legislatures, edited by Belle Zeller, appears under the title *American State Legislatures* (New York, Thomas Y. Crowell Company, 1954). This contains a useful bibliography on representation and apportionment. There is also a brief but well-organized chapter on the same subject, though it unfortunately contains numerous misleading statements. Richard Neuberger's *Adventures in Politics* (New York, Oxford University Press, Inc., 1954) includes an appraisal of a rural-dominated legislature from the viewpoint of an urban state senator (elected in 1954 to the United States Senate).

There have been numerous accounts of legislative representation in particular states. Among the best are: Thomas S. Barclay, "The Reapportionment Struggle in California in 1948," *Western Political Quarterly*, 4:313–24 (June

1951); Dean E. McHenry, "Urban v. Rural in California," *National Municipal Review*, 35:350–54, 388 (July 1946); and portions of Dayton McKean's *Pressures on the Legislature of New Jersey* (New York, Columbia University Press, 1938). Numerous monographs are available dealing with reapportionment problems in specific states, though these are usually limited in scope to constitutional and historical considerations. Among the better state studies are: *Legislative Apportionment in Oklahoma* (Norman, Okla., Bureau of Government Research, University of Oklahoma, 1951); Thomas Page, *Legislative Apportionment in Kansas* (University of Kansas Bureau of Government Research, 1952); and Alabama Legislative Reference Service, *Reapportionment* (1950).

The *National Municipal Review*, published monthly by the National Municipal League, is invaluable for students of state legislative representation. Not only does the *Review* publish frequent articles on the problem, but it also carries news briefs which keep abreast of current developments in the various states. Guthrie S. Birkhead compiled an excellent list of references on state representation under the title, "Legislatures Continue to Be Unrepresentative," *National Municipal Review*, 41:523–25 (November 1952). The best journalistic account of unbalanced representation is a series of three articles by Gus Tyler under the title "The House of Un-Representatives" in the *New Republic* for June 21, June 28, and July 5, 1954.